"I always wanted to write a book on angels. But I have to give up that ambition; Judith MacNutt has created such a beautiful piece of work that I dare not go there! Her book will be of great encouragement to all Christians."

Dr. R. T. Kendall, bestselling author; minister (retired),
Westminster Chapel, London

"Judith MacNutt has been collecting accounts of angels for years. This book enables us to share with her the riches of that collection, challenging the secular assumption that supernatural beings do not exist. Angels do exist and are very involved in human life. Praise God! And thank you, Judith."

Charles H. Kraft, professor emeritus,
Fuller Theological Seminary

"Everyone needs to know one basic truth: God the Father loves us. He cares for us, watches over us and blesses us. The ministry of angels is a real dimension of God's providence and love. Judith spells out this truth in a wonderful way. This is not theology, theory, teachings . . . but actual stories and experiences of God intervening in people's lives through angelic presence. Angels make real the love of God for His children. This is a very uplifting and affirming book for all of us."

Father Richard McAlear, oblate missionary,
Oblates of Mary Immaculate

"Judith MacNutt brilliantly illuminates the wonders of God's provision through His angels. The focus is not on the sensational, but on the everyday majesty of how He truly never leaves us nor forsakes us. Judith hands us a fresh lens for recognizing His messengers and praising God for them."

Allison Bown, author, *Joyful Intentionality*;
director, The Warrior Class

ENCOUNTERING
Angels

ENCOUNTERING

TRUE STORIES *of* HOW THEY TOUCH OUR LIVES EVERY DAY

JUDITH MACNUTT

Chosen
a division of Baker Publishing Group
Minneapolis, Minnesota

© 2016 by Judith MacNutt

Published by Chosen Books
11400 Hampshire Avenue South
Bloomington, Minnesota 55438
www.chosenbooks.com

Chosen Books is a division of
Baker Publishing Group, Grand Rapids, Michigan

Printed in the United States of America

Some names and identifying details of individuals described in this book have been changed in order to protect their privacy.

Library of Congress Control Number: 2015952330

ISBN 978-0-8007-9780-5

Unless otherwise indicated, Scripture taken from the HOLY BIBLE, NEW INTERNATIONAL VERSION®. Copyright © 1973, 1978, 1984 Biblica. Used by permission of Zondervan. All rights reserved.

Scripture quotations identified KJV are from the King James Version of the Bible.

Cover design by LOOK Design Studio

16 17 18 19 20 21 22   7 6 5 4 3 2 1

To Rachel and David,
my beloved daughter and son.
Remembering rainy-day pops and sheet tents;
treks in England, cream tea and caterpillar cakes;
unending bedtime stories,
dress-up days and the magic of holidays;
discovering the wonder of nature,
and the wonderment of childhood;
experiencing the miracle of God's love in our family!
We have grown in the shelter of one another,
always loving with His love and forgiving with His grace.
You have enlarged our hearts with your love
and infused us with life and enormous joy.
You are remarkable and unique individuals
stamped with His nature,
wrapped in His love and given as gifts.
God graced us with His best!
I love you.

Contents

Acknowledgments   11

Introduction   15

1. Children's Guardian Angels   23
2. Guardian Angels Sent to Protect   47
3. Angels Bring Comfort   67
4. Messenger Angels   87
5. Angels Encourage Worship   107
6. The Presence of Angels at Death   121
7. Jesus: The Significance of Angels   151
8. Angels in the Life of Jesus   171
9. Angels and the Spread of the Gospel   193

Conclusion   215

Acknowledgments

I've learned that publishing a book requires a loving, supportive, talented community of family, friends and people I've never met but appreciate deeply. Actually writing the book is only a portion of the process to bring it into being.

Deep gratitude to my talented daughter, Rachel, who spent countless hours laboring over every detail of the book, from art design to editing and communication. You are enormously gifted by God! Your constant encouragement along with your inspired sticky notes and gallons of hot tea kept me motivated to continue. Even when your part was completed you stayed with me during the crunch time to make the deadline. You are an awesome, strong woman of God and a gifted writer. I give thanks for your faith in God, your enormous heart of love, mercy and compassion—and that you are my daughter. You are precious to me!

Many thanks to my talented son, David, who masterfully edited a hundred angel stories several times for readability and length. Your unswerving dedication provided enormous motivation to persevere. Your encouragement and wisdom lifted me beyond the frequent setbacks to the distant goal. Thank you for consistently reminding me of the value of persistence. Your video of an exhausting day writing will forever be my favorite! How blessed I am to have a son who treasures his faith, his family and God's path for his life. I love you!

To my husband, Francis, my dearest friend and loyal companion in this extraordinary journey. Your offerings of theological insight and extraordinary wisdom created a necessary balance as you edited numerous versions of the manuscript. Your constant love, prayers and gentle encouragement were invaluable. I couldn't have done this without you! I am privileged and blessed by God to be your life partner in the healing ministry. I have learned the power of love from living with you.

Many thanks to my friend Kathi Smith, who once again took my handwritten pages and turned them into a manuscript. You are a gift from God!

I'm very grateful to my longtime friend Lynne Sunderland for sharing her wonderful story of healing. You are a cherished friend whom I've trusted with all my secrets!

I was blessed tremendously with a great team in the final editing of the book, a main one being Gail Mosely. Your eye for detail caught many necessary changes, which created a much-improved book. Thank you! Another great member of the team was Sue Polsley, who read, critiqued and typed the final changes. You both added joy!

Many thanks to Jane Campbell, who once again encouraged me to believe that another book on angels would be beneficial. Also deep gratitude to Ann Weinheimer, my editor, whose expertise and giftedness made this a much better book. Many thanks to the talented professionals at Chosen Books who worked to bring this book into being.

Heartfelt thanks to the staff and board of CHM, especially Lee Ann Rummell, chair of the board, and Klodiana Lekaj, executive director, for shouldering the leadership of CHM while I was writing. You are both anointed women of God! To our CHM staff, our board of directors and our national advisory board, prayer ministers and intercessors—you are our beloved family in Christ. Francis and I are blessed to know you and serve God alongside you in this anointed ministry. We love you!

Thanks to the courageous people who contributed their angel encounters. Unfortunately, all of the stories submitted could not be used because of space; however, each story brought inspiration.

Many thanks to my friend Ann Riley for sharing her lovely beachside home, which provided a "time apart" for writing. Also to my dear friends Thad and Virginia McNulty, who continue to bless us with their friendship and their peaceful mountain home.

I have been blessed in my life with many friendships—you know who you are—and I hope you know how very much you mean to me! It is impossible to list all your names, but know that you are written in my heart. I love you all!

Introduction

> Make yourself familiar with the angels, and behold them frequently in spirit; for without being seen, they are present with you.
>
> Francis de Sales

After much prayer and deliberation, my friend and fellow psychotherapist, Lynne Sunderland, and I packed up or sold all our belongings, and moved to Jerusalem to open a house of prayer.

The vision the Lord gave us was to open a place where both Jews and Arabs could come to find the Prince of Peace, Jesus. We were provided a lovely, old Arab mansion that was donated to us for a few years by a Christian organization. We opened early every morning and stayed until late at night, sharing Scripture, prayer and food with anyone who came in seeking help.

During that time, Lynne had an amazing visit from an angel while living in Ecce Homo, a convent on the Via Dolorosa (The Way of the Cross) in East Jerusalem. We were in our midtwenties and blessed with a zealous faith and an earnest desire to share Jesus. We were not, however, blessed with any regular support from Christian groups back in the U.S. Somehow God always provided exactly what we needed but not any extra, so we had to be careful with our meager funds. Living in a convent was a great blessing because it was safe, clean, inexpensive and sacred. The nuns made us feel a part of their loving community, which meant a lot to us since we were not part of a mission group. Slowly we started meeting other Christians, and our circle of friends grew.

A very special friend was Floride, an older missionary who took us under her wing almost immediately. She shared her strong faith and boundless love with us. To this day, I thank God for her warm, nurturing presence and leadership in our lives. Through her unwavering encouragement and radical faith, we grew very quickly in our own spiritual journeys.

One Thursday evening, during a local interdenominational worship service, a young man approached the leaders, seeking prayer for his poor eyesight, which was deteriorating rapidly. He longed to be healed. After praying for him, Floride and I leaned over to Lynne, who could not see well either without her glasses, and challenged her to ask God to heal her eyes. Lynne looked startled at our suggestion and scoffed, saying, "If God wants to heal my eyes, He can break my glasses and tell me so." I told Lynne jokingly that I thought I felt a rumbling under my feet as she threw that remark toward heaven.

That evening we returned to the convent, said our devotions together and went to our separate bedrooms. Right before parting, I asked Lynne one more time if she would like prayer for her eyes. She shook her head and gave me the look that only best friends understand. As she walked to her room, I had a strong impression that something wonderful was about to happen.

Lynne went down the hall to her small room, which had a single bed with a nightstand next to it. Because the rooms were alongside an open courtyard surrounded by a high wall, we were advised by the nuns always to lock our doors before going to sleep.

The following is Lynne's account in her own words:

I locked myself in my room, prepared for bed and, as was my custom, read a psalm; then I placed my glasses on the small bedside table. I turned off the light and quickly fell asleep. The next morning I reached for my glasses and put them on. At first I was puzzled, then quite startled, when I discovered that both lenses had been shattered—an identical line ran from top to bottom in the center of each lens. I told myself that I must have dropped them in the night and picked them up again in my sleep. I dressed quickly and went to Judith's room.

Early that morning, I was awakened by Lynne pounding on my door. I rushed to open it, wondering what had happened. Lynne was standing there looking confused and perplexed, holding up a pair of glasses that appeared to be broken.

Now it was my turn to be confused. "What happened?" I asked. She explained excitedly how she had found the shattered lenses, and then she asked me if I had slipped into her room during the night. I said, "That wouldn't have been possible; you locked your door from the inside." Slowly it dawned on both of us that someone supernatural had visited Lynne in the night!

Please understand that this was difficult for us to comprehend. How could a being pass through a locked door and physically break the lenses of her glasses? Then I remembered Lynne's earlier quip: "If God wants to heal my eyes, He can break my glasses."

Lynne could not function well without glasses and had no means to replace them, so she asked sheepishly if I would be willing to pray that God would either heal her eyes or provide new glasses. We began praying daily for her healing.

Nearly two weeks went by without her being able to read, and she had a constant headache from eyestrain. She had no choice but to wait, pray and trust God.

On a Sunday morning, Lynne and I were sitting in a worship service at the Garden Tomb, listening to one of our favorite preachers, Jan Willem van der Hoeven. Suddenly Lynne was grabbing my arm, babbling, "I can see! I can see!" I looked at her glowing, smiling face and her tear-filled eyes, and realized that God had chosen this time to perform a miracle in her life.

In Lynne's words:

> During the service, I was distracted by the beauty of the Garden and not really listening to Jan Willem's sermon. As I was glancing around the Garden, one moment the flowers were a colorful blur, and the next moment the words on a sign on a tree across the Garden became crystal clear. I picked up a songbook and realized I could read the words clearly. The service was just ending as I grabbed Judith to share the miracle with her. As we were celebrating God's goodness, Mrs. Dobbie, the organist, made her way toward us. She asked, "What is God doing with you?" She explained that throughout

the service she could see a light around Judith and me, and she knew God was present and doing something.

A few days later, Dr. Robert Lindsey, our pastor at Narkis Street Baptist Church, heard about Lynne's healing and took her to an optometrist, where she had her eyes examined. After the examination, the doctor was incredulous that she had ever worn glasses—her vision was perfect.

Lynne relates:

Sometime later, when I learned that the young man who had sought healing for his vision had not been healed, I felt sad and confused. "Why me, Lord? I don't understand why my eyes and not his." As I sat quietly, I heard the Lord's gentle voice explain that more than just knowing "God so loves the world," I needed to understand and experience His great love for *me*.

I do not know if I have ever seen an angel, but I know that angels have visited my life with assignments from my heavenly Father, and that one night, while I slept, God's messenger came into my room and broke my glasses so that I might truly *see* God's love for me.

I am happy to report that the healing of Lynne's eyes lasted until she reached the age when most of us need glasses.

We are surrounded by an invisible dimension, a spiritual one, which is the dwelling place of angels, demons, saints and God. Every now and then, God permits us a glimpse into that realm, allowing us to see, hear or be touched by angels.

You might suddenly smell fragrant flowers in the middle of a cold, sterile environment, or hear a beautiful choir singing music not of this world. Perhaps you will feel a comforting hand on your shoulder and turn around but no one is there. Some might actually see a radiant, luminous angel who will reveal the depths of God's love and care during a difficult season of life. These encounters challenge us to open our hearts to the glorious reality of angels.

I believe angels are among us, bringing comfort, strength, healing, freedom and, most importantly of all, providing a stepping stone to the larger reality that is God's Kingdom—to the very heart of God.

In my previous book, *Angels Are for Real* (Chosen, 2012), I wrote in greater detail about what an angel is—what angels look like, their functions and about fallen angels. In this book, which covers new areas of the ministry of angels, I have included incredible, true-life stories of angelic visitations from people around the world and from all walks of life. Reading these accounts will increase your trust in God's love and the provision He has made for you as you journey through this life to eternity. I hope you will come to discover that these mighty angels are your earthly companions—friends on the journey of life. They bring peace, comfort, warning, protection and love as you move through challenging circumstances. They also enlighten your mind with truth and guidance from God, helping you to find your way.

As God enlarges your awareness of the spiritual realm, you will come to realize that these Kingdom beings are always with you in your personal journey, your family and your community. You are never alone; God has made provision for you. Anytime you feel lost, afraid, confused or desperate, you are probably focusing on your situation, not on God. As you turn to God for help, He releases His mighty angels to intervene supernaturally and come to your assistance.

It is my prayer that God will use this book of angelic encounters to bring you His encouragement, comfort and healing in the midst of the daily stresses and pressures of your life.

Dear Lord,

I thank You for Your deep, abiding love for me. Give me the gift of faith to entrust myself and all those that I love to Your tender care. Help me, with the gift of faith, to envision Your will and path for my earthly journey.

Lord, reveal to me what it meant when You came to be among us as a human being, like us in everything except sin.

Thank You for allowing me to see how very much You care for me by sending Your holy angels to be with me on this journey.

And just as when I was a child and had wide-open eyes of wonder, give me back those eyes to see the reality of the spiritual, unseen realm that surrounds me.

I thank You. Amen.

1

Children's Guardian Angels

> "See that you do not look down on one of these little ones. For I tell you that their angels in heaven always see the face of my Father in heaven."
>
> Matthew 18:10

Children have great value to God. Jesus seemed to be warning His listeners that God's angels are watching over "the little ones," as He referred to them, and that any behavior for or against them will be noted and judged.

In the Scripture above, Jesus focused attention vividly on the importance of respecting and guarding children. He also seemed to be indicating that each child has a guardian angel watching over him or her. When Jesus gathered the children in His arms and blessed them, ignoring the protests of His disciples, He set an example for us. Children and childlikeness are held in high esteem in the Kingdom of God. We are expected by God to protect, love and teach children.

From the moment of conception until we are guided to heaven at the end of our earthly journeys, our guardian angels accompany us. The following stories are powerful witnesses to the loving, protective care of our angels.

Seeing My Guardian Angel

As an Episcopal priest, I have seen angels sitting on a rafter in the church where I used to serve, especially when many of us were worshiping God. I became curious about my guardian angel, whom I had never seen, so I prayed, asking if I could have a glimpse of him.

A short time later, as I was driving across the connector to the island where my church was located, I saw him. I was thrilled. He looked to be about fifteen feet tall, and he was gliding effortlessly above the front of my car. He was holding a long rope in his hand that was attached to my car. I knew he was guarding me that day and always.

Later I asked the Lord if my angel had a name, and He spoke a name to me I had never heard before. I thanked my angel for protecting me, and I heard his reply in my spirit: He said he was following Jesus' orders, and that I should thank Jesus, not him. Since then, I do not talk to him. I just ask Jesus to please thank him for me. Once I asked the Lord if my guardian angel had been with me for a long time, and Jesus answered that he had been assigned to me since conception.

—Rev. Hazel L. Wilkinson, Ph.D.

So many elements of this story reveal deep truths regarding angels. We discover that angels love to participate in worship. As I write this, we just held our School of Healing Prayer and were aware of an unseen choir of angels joining us when we were singing in the Spirit during the healing service. Angels seem to be assigned to us at conception, so they are with us, providing a lifetime of care and companionship. Note the angel's reply to the priest when she thanked him. He said, "Thank Jesus, not me. I'm simply following Jesus' orders."

Allow me to focus mainly on Jesus' reply to this priest—that her guardian angel had been assigned to her at conception. This was definitely a radical discovery for her and something few people ever know.

My husband, Francis, and I wrote *Praying for Your Unborn Child* (Hodder and Stoughton, Ltd., 1988) as a result of what we had learned through our ministry. There are many Scriptures that convey the baby's active life in the womb. During healing prayer sessions, we have ministered to countless individuals concerning traumatic memories from this time in utero. In our research, we came to realize that the womb is the child's first world. What is experienced during those nine months in utero can deeply affect many significant areas of the child's future life. When God spoke to Jeremiah, the future great prophet, He said, "Before I formed you in the womb I knew you, before you were born I set you apart" (Jeremiah 1:5).

I knew a woman whose daughter was pregnant with her first child. This daughter came to visit her, so her mother put a rollaway in the corner of her own room for her daughter. The mother was worried about her daughter because she was having a difficult pregnancy. After going to bed, the mother prayed for an hour and then fell asleep. Later when she woke up, she saw a beautiful, large, glowing angel leaning over her sleeping daughter. Then she saw a small angel on the other side of the bed. She said, "Lord, who is that small angel for?"

God replied, *That's the angel for your daughter's unborn child—your grandchild.*

On another occasion, my husband and I were in Vail, Colorado, for an annual healing conference. Two of our friends were driving into Denver for the day, along with their pregnant daughter. Their daughter's friend was driving the car when they returned to Vail that night. The young girl, an inexperienced driver, lost control of the car on the icy road and it started to slide, but something stopped the car before it rolled down the mountain. A driver coming behind saw the incident and phoned for rescue. My friends knew without a doubt that they had been saved by God.

Now here is the fascinating part of the story. In Denver, they had the car washed, but in the snowy road conditions, the car had gotten dirty again. When the driver started to get back into the car, she noticed that there were handprints all over the side of the car that was by the edge. The handprints were huge, except for one set that was very small. They were all standing there, looking at those huge handprints, and the girl—who was not a believer—said, "Those were angels." Then she said, "Why are those small prints there?" And, just as in the earlier story with the pregnant woman, we believe it was an angel assigned to the unborn child who left the smaller prints.

These two stories indicate that angels are assigned to guard children even in the womb against anything that could harm them. In *Praying for Your Unborn Child*, Francis and I wrote about the need to pray daily for the child forming within the mother, not only for the child's physical and emotional development, but for protection from any harm.

> For you [God] created my inmost being; you knit me together
> in my mother's womb. I praise you because I am fearfully
> and wonderfully made; . . . my frame was not hidden from
> you when I was made in the secret place. When I was woven
> together in the depths of the earth, your eyes saw my un-
> formed body.
>
> Psalm 139:13–16

From these stories and Scriptures we are encouraged to
consider the deep, creative intimacy between God and the
emerging life of the unborn child. This embryo is not a random group of cells, but is already a beloved soul of God
who is knit together by His loving hand. This truth is seen
in the joyful reaction of John the Baptist in the womb of his
elderly mother, Elizabeth, when Mary greeted her. Elizabeth
was filled instantly with the Holy Spirit (see Luke 1:41).
Since life begins at conception, we should not be surprised
to find that a mighty guardian angel is assigned to us at the
moment of conception and remains with us throughout our
earthly journey.

When we are born into this noisy, spacious world, leaving behind the warmth and security of our mother's womb,
we carry deep within our spirit some knowledge of the unseen world. Roderick MacLeish describes this charmingly
in *Prince Ombra* (Random House, 1999): "It is said and is
true, that just before we are born an angel puts his finger to
our lips and says, 'Hush, don't tell what you know.' This is
why we are born with a cleft on our upper lips."

A memory returns to me from years ago when I was bath-
ing our daughter, Rachel. At her birth she was a bright, beautiful, inquisitive baby. She consumed the surrounding world
with her larger-than-life blue eyes, but she seemed often to
be gazing joyfully at someone just behind my shoulder. She

was definitely interacting with someone, as she was giggling happily. This would sometimes go on for several minutes. I would often become aware of a warm presence at my back, such as you might feel with someone standing close.

Was Rachel's guardian angel making sure she was not afraid of being in the hands of a nervous first-time mother? Many parents have told me similar stories about their babies reaching for someone, listening intently or responding happily to something unseen. Can we conclude from this evidence that babies and young children frequently see into the unseen? And if so, when is that ability lost? Can that vision and awareness be regained? Can it be that the angelic encounters are stamped in our memories from the very beginning of our lives and remain in our remembrance? "Deep calls to deep" (Psalm 42:7). It seems that the Holy Spirit wants to bring to mind those long ago spiritual connections, those times when we were gifted to see into the supernatural realm. Perhaps parents should encourage their children to remain attentive to those innate abilities so that spiritual awareness is not lost.

The following story illustrates the importance of teaching children to remain aware of their guardian angels throughout their lifetimes.

Through the Eyes of a Child

I always taught my five children the importance of the assistance of their guardian angels. Each night when we said our prayers together as a family, we recited a prayer known and loved by many Christians.

Angel of God, my guardian dear,
to whom God's love commits thee here,

Ever this day be at my side,
to light, to guard, to rule and guide.

The children seemed to take great comfort in knowing that someone was watching over them at all times. One morning I went around our home to wake up each child for breakfast. My beautiful little four-year-old daughter, Beth, was lying quietly in her bed, wide awake, staring at something near the side of her bed. Since she was usually the first one up, I became concerned that she might be sick, so I asked, "Beth, are you okay?"

Nodding her head yes, and clutching the sheet up under her chin, she quietly whispered, "He is here."

I asked, "Honey, who is here?"

In a hushed voice she answered, "You know, the one you told me about."

By this time, I was beginning to realize that Beth might be talking about a visit from her guardian angel. I inquired, "What does he look like?"

She exclaimed with excitement, "He was so bright, Mommy, and so very beautiful. He was smiling at me the whole time. He had on shiny armor with a helmet on his head and a big sword on his belt!" She said he was kneeling next to her bed when she woke up. I asked what she did when she realized he was her guardian angel. She demonstrated how she had put her head under the covers to hide. She said, "I peeked out two times and he was still there. But the third time I peeked out he wasn't there."

This experience had a profound effect on our family, but especially on Beth. Beth is now an adult with two lovely children of her own. Recently while visiting with her we were reminiscing about her childhood angelic vision and wondering what impact it had in her life. We thought perhaps God wanted Beth to know that she is always protected. Beth is now a law enforcement officer and her husband is a deputy sheriff, so they daily encounter many dangerous assignments. Beth believes her guardian angel wanted to assure her at an early age that she would never have to fear the possible consequences of her chosen career. She knows she is never alone.

—Barbara Shlemon

Many deeply spiritual people live their entire lives never seeing an angel, yet God opened Beth's eyes to allow her to see her angel and to understand His great provision for her safety.

In *Parochial and Plain Sermons* (Ignatius Press, 1997), Cardinal Newman wrote:

Though they are so great, so glorious, so pure, so wonderful, that the very sight of them (if we are allowed to see them) would drop us to the earth, as it did the prophet, Daniel, holy and righteous as he was, yet they are our fellow-servants and our fellow-workers, and they carefully watch over and defend even the humblest of us.

Deep Sea Angel

While visiting the beach with my family when I was seven, I swam too far out into the sea and became hopelessly caught in a riptide flowing into deeper parts of the ocean. My struggles to free myself from the current were futile. My parents were unaware I had gone out beyond the shallows and could not hear my screams. Just as I began to panic, an incredibly strong man appeared and pulled me out of the water. He carried me to shore, and then walked me back to where my parents were sitting on the beach (the riptide had carried me quite a ways down the shoreline).

I ran to my dad and gave him a hug of joy and relief, but neither of my parents could see the man behind me. When I told my dad what had happened, he went to look for the man to thank him, but no such man was to be found. I know now that my mysterious rescuer was an angel sent to save me from a certain death. His strength when bringing me back to shore was beyond normal strength and felt miraculous to me even as a child. He got me out of the water quickly, and his presence was sweet and calming. He seemed to have one purpose: to return me to my family safely. My experience that day continues to remind me that the Lord has a purpose for me. *Guardian angel* is a term I have since appreciated.

—Juli Catlin

As we become aware of angelic intervention in the day-to-day lives of the children in our care, our fears lessen. When I was teaching on angels during the Christmas season a few years ago, a young mother of four approached me and confided quietly that she felt a powerful release of the fears about her children as I was teaching. She said, "Now I can pray that God will send His mighty angels to guard them."

Most people can sympathize with the mother's concern in the following story about leaving her young daughter in the care of a relatively new friend.

Angel Protects Children

When my daughter was very young, I joined a weekly playgroup with two other mothers I had met at a Bible study. We took turns being host; the time was designed to give us two hours of free time while giving the children a chance to play with each other. This particular week one of the other mothers was hosting, so I went to drop off my three-year-old, Clare.

When we arrived at her lovely two-story brick home, the host offered to take me on a tour. When I walked into the playroom on the second floor, I noticed that the open windows did not have screens. I was concerned about our children playing in that room, but assumed they would be well supervised. I said a silent prayer of protection, asking the Lord to send holy angels to watch over them.

I left to enjoy my two hours of freedom, but felt uneasy about those open windows. I decided to return early to check on Clare. Pulling into the driveway, I spotted immediately some of the children leaning out the playroom window, which was directly over the concrete driveway. I began to panic, but then I saw something else—a huge, translucent angel standing in front of the window. The angel was two stories tall, and had positioned her body to block the open window—there was simply no way the children could fall out.

I had always prayed for angels to protect Clare, so this was truly an answer to prayer. The memory of that magnificent angel is as vivid now as it was when it happened many years ago.

—Patti Little

This remarkable angelic protection serves as a dramatic reminder of how God answers our heartfelt prayers for children. The huge, translucent angel blocked the open window with her own body. Imagine the comfort Patti felt realizing that when she is away from her daughter, a mighty angel is guarding her.

A common thread in many of these stories is the fact that a hasty prayer for a child is uttered at the moment of danger—and an angel responds. Without a doubt the angels assigned to protect children are present, whether we can see them or not, as the following story indicates.

An Angel Rescues Jesse

Jesse, my son, was nine years old. Had he been a cat, he would have been on his sixth life. My husband was in the navy, and we were living on a military base. One day, as Jesse was supposedly playing upstairs in his room, I heard him scream. The noise seemed to be coming from outside, so I hurried into the yard. What I saw next made my heart drop into my stomach—there was my son hanging from the two-and-a-half-story roof by his fingertips.

"Help, Mom! I can't hold on!"

"Jesse!" I cried out, desperately trying to think of what to do. Rushing back into the house, I scooped up a couch cushion and dashed back outside. All the while I was yelling, "God, help us!"

Within moments, unable to hold on any longer, he began falling toward the concrete driveway. Miraculously, when he was halfway to the ground, his deadly descent slowed in speed to a gravity-defying float. His body, featherlike, drifted down the rest of the way, and he landed softly on his feet. I could not believe what I had just seen.

Still in shock, I ran to him, took him into my arms and gave him a quick examination. There was not a scratch on him—he was perfectly fine.

What he said next left me simply dumbfounded. "Thanks for catching me, Mom."

"I didn't catch you," I said, "but someone did." I thank God for Jesse's strong guardian angel.

—Dixie Gordon

"God, help us!" This brief, desperate cry of a frightened mother brought the angelic rescue her son needed. Unseen arms caught Jesse and gently floated him safely to the ground. I have often mused that some children's guardian angels might ask God for a reassignment—as they are kept too busy!

A longtime friend of ours named Susan is threatened by the enemy after ministering freedom to a woman in need.

Sandbox Angel

I was attending an annual Christian Healing Ministries conference in the Northeast as part of the prayer team when my daughter was quite young. At the Friday night healing service, I was praying for deliverance and healing for a woman who was struggling with evil and was deeply agitated. The prayer had felt like a long battle, and though she was exhausted, the woman found healing and freedom through Jesus Christ.

Later as I was walking back to my hotel room, I suddenly felt extremely cold. I then felt a dark presence oppressing me with threatening taunts: *You are going to regret what you did tonight.* I had the distinct impression that my three-year-old daughter, Sarah, would be the enemy's target. Upon reaching my room, I fell to my knees, weeping. I asked Jesus to protect my precious daughter and me. As I continued to pray, deep peace filled me. I thanked God that He surrounds us with His warring angels.

The next day I went to pick up Sarah, who had been playing at a friend's house. As I walked into the backyard, I stopped in my tracks. Sarah was happily playing in the sandbox. Standing right behind her was a powerful-looking angel. He appeared to be ten feet tall, very masculine with broad shoulders. He had large wings and wore a white robe. I could not see his face, as he was facing Sarah. It was clear to me he was on an assignment to protect her. My eyes filled with tears as I picked her up and gave her the biggest hug. Seeing my tears, Sarah asked: "Mommy, are you okay?"

"Yes, sweetie," I replied. "I just love you so much."

—Susan Stanford-Rue, Ph.D.

Have you ever briefly lost track of the whereabouts of a child? It is a terrifying experience. The following account is about the little girl named Clare (whom we met earlier in the story about the playgroup), her frantic mother and giant guardian angels overseeing the entire neighborhood.

Neighborhood Angels

Several years ago, a paperboy was abducted in our neighborhood, and the crime is still unsolved.

Right after it happened, when parental fear was at its height, I had a frightening experience involving Clare. Our neighborhood consisted of homes with many small children who had the freedom to play in each other's yards.

One afternoon I could not find her. I searched everywhere. Soon our neighbors joined the search. There was no trace of her. In desperation I called 911, and a policeman arrived quickly at our home.

While I was talking to the officer, a neighbor finally found Clare under a daybed in our family room, hiding, huddled against the wall.

Later that day, as I was thanking God for Clare's safety, I was allowed to see angels surrounding our neighborhood. I saw them rising above the trees, where they had a panoramic view of the area. The angels conveyed deep, peaceful assurance, which enabled me to release my fears. I have never seen them again, but I still feel their presence.

—Patti Little

Three Angels for Three Children

Ever since I can remember, I have been aware that a guardian angel is present in my life. Growing up I used to say, "If it were not for my guardian angel . . ." One time in particular I decided to play King of the Mountain by climbing up on top of an oil drum. When I reached the top of the drum, it toppled over and crashed onto my forehead. As heavy as the drum was, it barely injured me. I am convinced that an angel protected me from a concussion by breaking the drum's fall.

My most memorable experience of angels, though, came when I was a young mother of three beautiful children. One night, during my prayer time, I opened my eyes to see three wavy white figures appear and continue to float over me for fifteen minutes. I was awestruck and did not move.

Then one angel lifted me up and took me to each child's room. As I prayed over my children, the angels blessed them. Suddenly I was back in my bedroom, lying next to my sleeping husband. I was fully awake and still praying. I knew what I had experienced was real, but for years I hesitated to share this story.

—Linda Crofton

What is striking about this mother's vision is the awareness that three angels appeared to her—one for each of her children—while she was praying. When we are focusing our full attention on God, we become receptive to the spiritual realm that surrounds us. As we yield our fears to God, He sometimes graces us to see our children's guardians.

Guardian angels provide protection for children in dangerous situations; however, they can also bring peace, comfort, strength and sometimes much-needed rest. This next story is from our friend Virginia, who longs for more of God's supernatural presence at her boarding school.

Angels in the Chapel

After I finished studying for my courses one weekend, I called my mom. I told her that we were going to have a confirmation service during chapel, and I was not looking forward to attending. The topics chosen for chapel often seemed negative and left me feeling down. My mom suggested that I pray for an angel to show up during chapel.

For a moment, the idea stunned me. Then I thought, *Why not?* I prayed, "Lord, please bring Your heavenly angels and reveal Your great power and glory today in chapel. That would be a crazy intervention that this school needs."

That night at the service, I paid more attention to my surroundings than to the actual ceremony because I really expected angels to appear. I wondered what an angel would look like.

No angels appeared that night. The following week, however, something special did happen. As I was praying in my room, I had a vision of the chapel, which is a large Gothic structure—beautiful, but cold. In the vision, I was in the balcony, looking down toward the front. Two angels appeared, standing side by side. They rose, growing taller, until they were about twenty feet tall. As they rose, their wings extended slowly to cover the full width of the chapel. Their wingspan overlapped in the middle of the front stage. They looked human, with solid bodies, but with silvery skin. They wore beautiful white robes. I believe God gave me this vision to show me that He had assigned angels to the chapel to protect and guide us.

—Virginia Smith

This story is a good example of a devout young lady who longed to experience the depths of God's presence. Like many young people seeking God, her experiences at chapel left a negative impression on her. God sent Virginia reassurance of His presence through this powerful vision of His holy angels.

The loss of a loving friendship can be devastating for anyone, but especially for a teenager. During those years, a faithful friend can help guide and support through the maze of conflicting emotions, temptations and pressures. For Lily, this loss draws her into darkness from which only God and His angel can rescue her.

Radiant Light for a Lost Soul in the Dark

Even though I have many friends, there is one person whom I consider to be my best and truest. Tara and I met while attending a small-town high school in the far south of California. She spent so much time at my home that she became like a sister. We had a fun and supportive relationship.

This singular friendship was a dream come true for a high-schooler, but it turned into a crushing weight the day that Tara told me that she would be moving away in only two days' time. I began to cry and asked her why she had not told me sooner. "I was praying," she said, "but I couldn't postpone telling you any longer."

"We'll still be friends, though, right?"

"Of course! We're sisters, remember?"

On her last night in town, she stayed at my house. The next morning her parents arrived to pick her up. My best friend was leaving. The reality was more than I could bear. I began to sob uncontrollably. As I watched the car pull away, it seemed as though my tears would never stop.

After that day I entered into a spiritual and emotional darkness that seemed to eclipse all the good in my life. I could feel myself sinking into despair. Before long I had become self-destructive. I began to stay out late and party hard with new friends. Most of my time was spent getting high.

During this "dark night" of my life, Tara texted me three simple words, but it opened my heart: "I miss you."

I never considered myself religious, but that night I sobbed while I prayed to God, asking Him to bring my sister home. Then, remembering half-heard Sunday school lessons, I repented for my destructive choices. I begged Him to forgive and cleanse me. I fell asleep with my face on my tear-soaked pillow.

The next morning, I woke up feeling that something strange was happening in my room. A brilliant light was only three feet from the foot of my bed. I stared at the light, completely in awe of its beautiful brilliance. A short time later, the light began to fade.

Suddenly I felt peaceful, cleansed and happy for the first time in months. I then realized that I was not reaching for my usual morning cigarette. When I had started hanging out with the bad crowd, I had become addicted to cigarettes; I usually smoked two when I woke up. Yet now I did not want one! I smiled as I realized that my prayer had been answered. I began to cry again, but this time my tears were joyful. I began thanking and praising God. I would never again doubt His power and presence in my life.

Was the radiant light an angel sent to heal me? That holy presence marked the replacement of the pain and anger in my life with newfound love, peace, hope and happiness.

A year after that life-changing experience, the doorbell rang. I opened the door to see—to my amazement—Tara, with a big grin on her face. I screamed with happiness. She delivered the good news that she was back in town for good. I was endlessly grateful to God for bringing my best friend home and for freeing me completely from my addictions—and showing me His great love.

—Lily Gonzalez

Following Lily's desperate prayers and repentance, God sent a brilliant angel of light to release her from the destructive path of an addictive life. Instead of shame and guilt, Lily found God's forgiveness, and His restoration of her peace, joy and—one year later—her best friend!

Over the years in family counseling sessions, I have listened to many guilt-ridden parents who have allowed their anger toward their children to get out of control. Stressful situations in many of our homes cause this anger. Unhealed wounds from childhood and dysfunctional ways of expressing anger can also contribute to these outbursts. The following story serves as a piercing reminder of our obvious need to rely on God's abundant grace in caring for children.

An Angel's Reaction to a Mother's Anger

Due to a stressful day, I lost my temper with our three sons as they were preparing for bed. My anger was spinning out of control, and sadly, I was directing most of my critical words toward our eldest son,

Mercer. I ended my tirade with something like, "All of you get into your rooms and into bed, *now*!"

After I calmed down, I proceeded to go to each child's room to say bedtime prayers. Nathan shared a room with his identical twin, Sam. As Nathan snuggled with his white stuffed bunny, he said, "Mommy, do you know what Mercer's guardian angel does when you yell at him?"

Surprised, I said, "No. What does he do?"

Nathan said, "He kneels down between you and Mercer and prays, 'God, please help her stop yelling at Mercer.' Mommy, I know Mercer upsets you, but you don't have to get so mad. It hurts God and the angels . . . and Mercer."

Totally convicted by this simple truth and with tears running down my face, I said, "I was wrong. Thank you for telling me what you saw."

Nathan said, "Mommy, you need to go tell Mercer you're sorry."

When I got to Mercer's room, he was crying. He said, "Mommy, I know I'm bad. But you don't have to yell at me so mean."

Grieved, I asked for Mercer's forgiveness after telling him how sorry I was for yelling at him and his brothers. Thank God for His holy angels.

—Joe Carol Thorp

Visualize for a moment a mighty radiant angel of God kneeling in prayer between a frightened child and his angry mother. While shielding Mercer from the effects of the negative words, the angel was also imploring God to make it stop.

One of the many roles angels play in our lives is to protect and shield us from harm. The angel's prayer brought grace, peace and forgiveness into this family. Nathan, who was allowed to see Mercer's angel, was able to help his mother understand how her anger had caused such sadness.

Perhaps as you read this story, a time came to your mind when your anger was out of control, a time when you wounded a child, spouse or friend, causing a rupture in your relationship. Memories such as these remind each of us of our broken humanity and our tremendous need for the healing power of God and His love in our relationships. During these times we should remember that we have angels praying for us.

A beloved granddaughter is in a dangerous, life-threatening situation, but her grandmother, sensing the need, begins to intercede for heaven's helpers.

A Grandmother's Prayer

When I was thirteen, I went to the beach with a friend's family. The first two days we were disappointed because the weather was rainy and cold. On the third day, when the sun finally came out, my friend and I ignored warnings about dangerous tidal currents and went straight out into the big waves. Meanwhile, back at home, my grandmother, with whom I am very close, was praying for me because she felt that something was not right.

As we thrashed around in the huge waves, my friend and I got separated, and I found myself alone in the raging sea. She was yelling to me that I had gone out too far. I looked toward shore and saw that it was very far away. When I realized that I could not touch the sea floor, I began to scream. I could hardly breathe as the waves crashed over my head and began to pull me under. I thought I was going to die.

Out of nowhere, a girl my age swam up behind me and said, "You will be okay. Give me your hand." After I grabbed her extended hand, she gently pulled me to shore. Back on the sand, coughing and crying, I looked up to thank her but could not find her anywhere. I truly believe this was my guardian angel protecting me.

—Jessica McClellan

Jessica was gently but surely led to the safety of shore by an angel in the guise of a teen, speaking comfort and peace to her. Thank God for praying grandmothers!

"The angel of the LORD encamps around those who fear him, and he delivers them" (Psalm 34:7). This is a wonderful image of angels around us, protecting us. Every night and every morning we should ask God to send His holy angels to protect us and those we love.

In the next story, a family tragedy is averted by the quiet, unobtrusive presence of a guardian angel in human form appearing at just the right moment.

Toddler Saved by an Angel

When I was a toddler, I loved to play in the driveway of our home, forming the pebbles into a makeshift sandbox. One morning my father came rushing out of the house, jumped into his car and threw it into reverse without seeing me. Just before he was about to back the car right over me, he saw a man in the rearview mirror. The man was looking at him and pointing down to where I was sitting. My father, curious, got out and found me, oblivious, playing in the pebbles. He was mortified, and grateful that the man had passed by just at that moment and alerted him to my presence.

Many years later, when my father and I were having lunch, I asked him about that day. I was curious to know if he had thanked the man for saving me. "No," he said. "When I got out of the car he was gone." We looked at each other quizzically, because it had just occurred to both of us that no one could move out of sight in the few seconds it took for my dad to get out of his car. Our only conclusion is that God sent an angel to warn my dad to avert a horrible accident.

—Karen Alban

Many stories of angelic assistance reveal that once the assignment is completed, the angel disappears. Karen and her father did not recognize until years later that the man who saved her life was an angel of God.

God's eyes and His tender, loving gaze are on us from the beginning of our existence. In addition, He provides mighty guardian angels to watch over us for the remainder of our lives, even into eternity.

2

Guardian Angels Sent to Protect

God our Father
You are the Lord of love and mercy.
Place Your kindness in us.
Change our hearts into vessels of Your love.
Send Your mighty angels of peace
To enlighten and console us
Along every step of our journey to Your wait-
　　ing arms.
Amen.

This ancient prayer of the Church emerged during the Middle Ages in Europe. The vast majority of Christians found great comfort in the Church's teaching that each person has a guardian angel assigned at conception to give protection on his or her earthly journey. In our time, reports abound of powerful beings of light or mysterious strangers appearing to rescue someone from danger. I have collected angel stories for many years, and the evidence indicates overwhelmingly that guardian angels are very active in human affairs, as the following story will suggest.

An angel in human form is found in the most unlikely place—seated next to a young woman as she travels late into the night and into a dangerous situation.

Angel on a Greyhound Bus

My sister, Barbara, pregnant with her first child, was traveling home to Alabama from Winter Haven, Florida. After changing buses in Tallahassee, she was due to arrive in Dothan, Alabama, at four p.m. In Tallahassee, she missed her connection and had to wait for the next bus, which would get her to Dothan at midnight.

Meanwhile, in Dothan, our pastor and his wife had taken our mother to the bus station to meet her. When Barbara did not arrive, they asked an agent in Tallahassee to page her to give her the message to stay in Tallahassee and take the bus to Dothan the following day instead of arriving late. She did not receive the message, so she took the next bus to Dothan. Shortly after the boarding announcement, a lady sat down beside her at the station. My shy sister did not talk with her other than to ask where she was going, which happened to be to the same destination.

When they boarded the bus, the lady again sat down next to Barbara. They did not talk during the trip, but Barbara remembers feeling comfortable and safe with her. Later that night, arriving in Dothan, they were the only people left waiting in the dark. She thought it was odd that there was no one there to meet the woman, but she did not give it much thought at the time. She was more concerned about how she was going to get home herself, since no one was there to meet her either.

She saw one car remaining in the parking lot, with a man sitting inside. He approached Barbara and asked her if she needed a ride home. She climbed into the front seat and the woman slid in beside her. She said it made her feel safer.

The man reached over and placed his hand on Barbara's leg. She immediately jerked away. They kept a tense silence for the rest of the ride. She was very scared.

Arriving at her home, Barbara and the woman jumped out of the car. Still shaken, Barbara watched the car speed off into the night. She turned to thank the woman for remaining with her, but the woman had disappeared.

I am sure my mother did not sleep much that night and had been praying for God's angel to bring her daughter safely home!

—Kathryn Hickman

A deeply concerned mother prayed for the safety of her daughter. Heaven responded by sending a "lady" to accompany Barbara on that midnight journey, offering comfort, peace and safety. When the woman's charge was safely home, the angel vanished.

Angels in a Dream

One of my first encounters with angels came when I was a new, Spirit-filled believer of less than a year.

I was visiting a woman I consider holy. We were in her kitchen, when suddenly the screen door opened and shut by itself. This door was the kind on which the spring would squeak as it opened and then bang when it closed. I saw no one come into or leave her home, and so I asked about it. Her response was that it must have been an angel.

As soon as she finished saying that, a vision from my dream of the previous night came flooding into my spirit. In this vision I was on a mountaintop, and I could see a long distance, as if I had binocular eyes. I was also aware of a strong, peaceful presence standing beside me with his arm around my shoulders. I could see his garments flashing like lightning, but I was too scared to look at his face. Finally, when I looked up, I felt all my strength leave me and I fell to the ground. I felt as if my whole body was numb and no longer under my control. This being placed his hands on my shoulders, and I immediately stood upright.

He spoke and said he wanted to show me certain aspects of my life, so he turned me to face three enormous semi-opaque screens. It was like watching home movies—the one on the left was my past, the middle one was present events, and the right screen was future ones. The far right one was blurry—like 3D without wearing glasses. As he spoke about things in my life, his language changed; before, I heard him speak in English, but then it became a strange language that somehow I could comprehend.

At the end of this encounter he told me that I had other angels watching over me, and immediately two more appeared in front of me. One had a dark complexion and carried a long spear. He also had a sling over his shoulder that carried a bow and arrow. When I looked at him, I could not make out his face, but he felt like a force of protective good. I could not see him visually but was keenly aware of his presence and the power that he brought in my spirit. All of this came flooding back visually to me in the kitchen, and, overwhelmed by what I saw, I fell off the chair.

—Robin Morrison

A caring minister watches, as if in slow motion, a woman about to be run over by a car and offers a quick, powerful prayer.

Lifted by an Angel

One autumn, when my wife, Betty, and I were part of a prayer team, we were ministering at a lovely house in rural England. At the end of the day I went outside for a breath of air. The house was situated on the edge of a narrow lane with high banks on either side and a gated entrance.

Standing there, I was watching the lights of a car that was winding its way along the foot of the hill in front of me. Behind me I heard the front door of the house open. The young woman we had been praying with went tearing past me in an agitated state. Despite my warning, she went running down the hill as if she were being chased by a swarm of bees. Before I could run after her, I could see that the approaching headlights of the car were almost upon her. My only recourse was to pray a hasty prayer that the angels would grab her.

The next few seconds were almost unbelievable. As I watched with horror at what appeared to be the unfolding of an inevitable accident, the woman was plucked right out from the middle of the lane, as if an invisible hand had grabbed her in midstride. Before my eyes she was lifted up against the bank just as the car swung round the bend. I doubt if the driver was even aware of her presence.

In that moment I knew the angels had rescued her. I am sure that there are many times in our lives when we are helped by angels but are completely unaware of their assistance.

—Ronald Bisset

Invisible hands of a mighty angel plucked this woman up like a child, putting her outside of harm's way. This angel responded to a short cry for help for a distressed woman in great need.

A tendency shared by most of us is to limit the activity of guardian angels to the care of small children. Numerous artists have portrayed children and angels, which contributes to this mistaken limitation. The following account focuses on the watchful angelic care of an elderly couple who needed protection.

Angels Amidst the Flames

As the McMillons, our neighbors, were getting ready for bed one cold, rainy winter night, Mrs. McMillon cautioned Ernest, her husband, that she smelled smoke. They had a fire burning in the fireplace to keep warm, but all of the smoke was supposed to exit through the chimney. Mrs. McMillon is blind, but her keen sense of smell warned her that all was not right.

Ernest stoked the dying fire and looked around for a possible burning ember that could have fallen out of the fireplace. He even poked around inside the chimney to see if he could detect anything. After adding another piece of wood to take the chill out of the air for their first hours in bed, he reassured his wife, Ola, that all was well with the fireplace. Trusting that the fire was contained, they went to sleep.

They fell asleep peacefully in their modest two-room home. They had a small bedroom fireplace, plus one in the kitchen that they used for cooking during the winter. The entire home was probably no more than eighteen by twenty feet, and the outside walls were patched with various pieces of scrap lumber and tin. There were no inside walls, which meant there was no insulation. There was a roof of sorts, but leaks in both rooms let in rain. There was no running water and no bathroom inside the house.

A year earlier, Curtis, a neighbor, had agreed to repair two of the worst leaks. When I saw him up on that unstable roof, I realized he was not only doing a neighborly favor; he was risking his life. One of the leaks was around the bedroom chimney, and he warned the McMillons that the roof was in bad shape. Mr. McMillon was in his eighties, almost blind, and was satisfied with his home regardless.

The following morning as Mr. McMillon awoke, he could immediately see with his limited vision that something was wrong. His roof was on fire, and day-light was streaming in through gaping holes around the chimney. They called the fire department, and neighbors rushed over.

Once out of the house, Mrs. McMillon kept say-ing, over and over, "The angels were watching over us, the angels were watching over us." As I write this now, I still get a chill, and a bit of a thrill, because I have to agree that the angels had indeed watched over them. The fire around the chimney had smoldered all night long, and had not spread more than a few inches. The firemen were amazed. The McMillons had slept in peace; they believe that angels tended the fire.

—Irene Ferguson

When we become increasingly aware of angelic activity in our lives, we sometimes need to reinterpret past events that we once labeled as mere coincidences, as the following stories suggest.

Carried by an Angel

When I was a teenager, a mysterious thing happened while I was cutting down a tree in the Blue Ridge Mountains of northern Georgia. When I had cut the tree almost all the way through, the trunk broke loose and fell toward me. In an effort to evade the falling tree, I jumped backward. It was a reflexive movement that would usually carry me only a few feet, but this time I managed to cover at least ten feet. It seemed as if I had flown.

Looking at the tree on the ground where I had been standing, I was puzzled about what had just happened. There had been no wind, and I had back-cut the trunk well, so there was no logical reason why it would have fallen toward me.

Years later, when I related this story to a Christian osteopathic navy flight surgeon, he told me that humans are not equipped with the muscles to jump backward more than a few feet. He felt that an angel had intervened to preserve me in what could have been a deadly accident. Now, having felt their protection firsthand, I believe angels are always looking after us.

—Joe Brundage

Saved by an Angel

My husband, Taylor, and I were on a Black Angus cattle ranch in Australia visiting a rancher friend, Mark. He had asked us to help him brand his cows. Being the city slickers that we were, we were very excited about experiencing something new. Little did we know what was about to unfold. A few minutes later we were in the pen with Zack the Cadillac (the name of their bull), who had lured all the female cows inside the pen so that Mark could then lead them through to the branding station.

Suddenly Mark screamed, "Get out, get out! There are two bulls in the pen and they are fighting!" I was able to exit quickly, but Taylor was cornered across the pen. The two bulls were fighting head to head, pounding in his direction. As the bulls roared toward the place where he was standing, he was able to swing his body over the eight-foot fence. He had less than two seconds before he was literally going to be crushed into the fence. After this very scary event, he tried to duplicate (unsuccessfully) his heroic jump over the fence to freedom. Was it adrenaline or was it an angel? I think an angel.

—Kathi Smith

Reflecting on this life-threatening experience years later, Kathi and Taylor concluded that an angel had saved his life. The many times that angelic interventions have changed one's destiny are often revealed later in life.

In the following story, a lovely Austrian ski trip becomes a disaster for one woman when the weather shifts. Her two visitors seem to provide that angelic response she needs for instant help.

Downhill Skier

I was in Austria on a ski trip in and around Innsbruck. Because we were going to new areas each day, I was generally unfamiliar with the terrain and trails. On the third day the weather started to decline quickly and unexpectedly, and I found myself on the top of a mountain in dangerous conditions. Being an experienced skier, I knew that I needed to get down the mountain as quickly as possible. I began my descent, but within a few minutes the weather worsened and I was skiing through white-out conditions. I could barely see my hand at only a foot away from my face, and a sense of vertigo set in so that I could not tell which way was up or down, making it dangerous to move. Austrian ski runs are narrower than in the U.S. and poorly groomed, making a bad situation worse. I stopped and stood there, freezing, as the weather continued to decline.

After a minute or two, I was surprised when two men appeared in front of me. It was hard to see them through the snow, and they were speaking a language that I did not recognize. One of the men beckoned with his hand for me to follow him. As he began to ski down the slope, I kept my skis right behind his. Staying focused only on his skis, I skied for what seemed like an eternity. He eventually slowed to a halt, and I realized that we had reached the bottom of the mountain. When I looked around with the intention of thanking them, the two men were nowhere to be found. I hurriedly made my way over to the lodge area nearby and continued to look for them there. There was no sign of them, nor had anyone in my group seen them come down with me.

I believe these men were angels sent to save my life that day. I will be forever grateful for the help I received.

—Kathe Hanson

Typical of angels in human form, the young men were not seen by anyone besides Kathe, and they disappeared when she was safely deposited at the bottom of the slope. Since that memorable day, Kathe has become increasingly aware of the angelic realm, even in her counseling practice. As she listens to her clients' experiences that cannot be explained, she joyfully reveals to them how the angels have intervened in her life.

I have heard a variety of stories where angels intervene and prevent car accidents—either a car careening out of control is stabilized or unseen hands grab the steering wheel at the last moment before impact.

Mysterious Driver

Several years ago I attended my first prayer meeting. I was always fearful of new situations and meeting new people. Although I felt the Holy Spirit prompting me to talk at the meeting, I could not. On my drive home, I was reviewing in my mind the reasons I could not speak, coming up with several excuses, none of which was valid.

I was driving a full-size conversion van that had bad brakes. Whenever I needed to stop, I gave myself extra space to slow down because the rear of the van would swing to the right whenever I applied the brakes. I was on a five-lane highway (with two eastbound lanes, two westbound and a center turn lane). I was in the left lane, passing a small pickup truck, when the truck began to veer into my lane. The driver did not see me. All I could manage to do was blow my horn and hit the brakes.

Instantly, my van was mysteriously steered into the center lane. Looking out my windshield, I saw a large angel with outstretched arms above my van. It took my breath away. I have no doubt that this was the angel who moved my van.

At that moment I resolved next time at the prayer group to share the story of God's loving protection.

—Marcia Moore, M.S.Ed., CJM, A

A mother and her young daughter delivering food baskets on Thanksgiving find themselves in need. After a brief but heartfelt prayer, an angel of God appears.

Red Tow Truck Angel

My husband, Mike, and I were in leadership of a Vineyard church in Denver, Colorado, called Church in the City. As Thanksgiving approached, we teamed with other churches to make holiday baskets for needy families. I was responsible for picking up the baskets.

I left my Bible study with my five-year-old daughter and headed to get the baskets. Snowfall had been heavy in recent days, and the unplowed roads made the drive slow. Running late, I decided to take a back-road short-cut to the pickup point. Seeing what appeared to be a sufficiently plowed road, I turned onto it.

Suddenly I saw a car coming toward me, so I veered to the right. It was a narrow road, and my tires sank into a small ditch. Unable to achieve trac-tion, my tires spun in vain. My daughter, Christen, was a little scared, but I assured her that everything was okay. I remember praying, "Oh, God, I could sure use a tow truck right now."

Moments after my quiet prayer, I was stunned to see a red tow truck driving down the little road. It was headed our way. As the truck pulled up, the driver rolled down his window and offered help. We were so relieved.

He hopped out of the truck, hooked my car's bumper to the cable and pulled the car out of the ditch. I thanked him and offered to pay him, but he declined, saying he was glad to help. As I started my car, I looked in my rearview mirror. The tow truck was gone! I looked in every direction and there was no truck in sight. I smiled and thanked Jesus—I knew I had been helped by an angel.

—Tina Wurschmidt

To my delight, I have countless stories of this angelic tow truck driver. He is kept very active on our highways rescuing needy and scared drivers.

The following supernatural encounter is between a "mechanic" and two men stranded on their way to a weekend outing.

Supernatural Encouragement

It only takes one supernatural encounter to shake you to your core and get you thinking.

We were eight guys, setting out for a weekend canoe trip in the Okefenokee Swamp near Fargo, Georgia. We were in four separate cars, with each vehicle toting its own canoe on top. We were all in our thirties, and all anxious to tackle the hard nine-mile run through dense swampland to Craven's Hammock.

I had been invited on this trip by a group of Christian guys who had something in their lives that appealed to me, but I was not quite sure what it was. I had grown up as a professed Christian, but had put God through some tough dances, enough that I figured He had probably given up on me.

John and I were cruising on Interstate 10, around thirty miles outside of Jacksonville, Florida, in John's car—my dream vehicle—an old International Scout, when the engine started making a loud clanking sound, as if it had thrown a rod. Fortunately, we were close to an exit, so we coasted off the interstate and into an old service station that had been converted into a mechanic's garage. What grabbed my attention was that it was painted light blue with a white dove on the front, exactly like John's front license plate.

A man came out to meet us, and he and John started talking Christianese. Then the guy asked if he could take the Scout for a spin down the road to get a sense of what was happening with the engine.

When the mechanic returned, he said that everything was working just fine. I was suspicious, but the engine did seem to be humming without a hitch. The mechanic would not take any payment, so we shook his hand and drove off.

A couple of weeks later, I was driving on the same interstate, so I decided to stop and thank the mechanic for helping us. When I turned into the place, all I saw was an old, dilapidated, faded white building with weeds in the parking lot. I stood there for a while, checking the intersection once more, confirming it was the same, then staring again at the same exact building, though it was now run-down and had been uninhabited for quite some time. I was completely baffled. I knew I had been at this place a few weeks earlier. Who was the accommodating man who miraculously fixed our car by driving it? Why was the station not blue with the white dove painted on it? Had it been a sighting of something divine? The only conclusion I could come to was that something miraculous had happened.

As a side note, several of the members of the camping group, including John, invited me to join them at a men's Bible study, and I accepted. Within a year I entered a much deeper personal relationship with Christ. My transformation was largely due to the spiritual encouragements of my faithful friends, but it grew also out of witnessing the mysterious and supernatural things that God can do to engage with us in our lives. I now consider that event glorious and supernatural.

—Skip Allcorn

Skip's supernatural encounter opened his eyes and his heart and led him to a deeper relationship with Jesus Christ. In addition to the unusual circumstances with the mechanic, the garage is part of the mystery!

Following a hazardous car incident, a woman's cry to God for help is answered in the form of an angel.

Angel in a Mustang

Angels come in all shapes and sizes, and apparently they sometimes use unexpected modes of transportation. I discovered this on my drive home from college one Friday evening. I had just finished an exhausting week at school and was looking forward to both my mom's cooking and my charismatic prayer meeting.

I was on the highways of Long Island, a notoriously busy road system. My '69 VW Beetle had no radio, so I passed time in traffic singing and praying.

About halfway through my journey, one of my tires blew out near one of the off-ramps. The sound of it rupturing and the loss of control were frightening. I managed to maneuver the car to a stretch of grass beside the highway. I was frightened and shaken, unsure of what to do. There were no phones or stores within walking distance.

Sunset was coming soon, so I decided to walk. I prayed, "Lord, either You send an angel to help me, or I'm going to start walking."

Within seconds of my eking out this prayer, a Ford Mustang pulled up. I was hopeful as a man stepped out. He opened the trunk, pulled out the spare and proceeded to change my tire without uttering a word. I knew in my spirit that this was the Lord answering my prayer.

When he finished, all I could manage through my tears was a feeble "Thank you." I rummaged through my purse and, finding a five-dollar bill, tried to hand it to him. He refused the money, saying simply, "You put that away. Next time you see someone in need, you help them." He turned, got back into his Mustang and drove off.

Overwhelmed with gratitude, I said, "Lord, You heard my prayer and sent a heavenly angel to change my flat tire—thank You." I had a great testimony to share at my prayer meeting that night.

—Geralyn Farley

Like most angels who appear in human form, her angel vanished from her sight quickly. Forty years later, Geralyn remains grateful to God for His loving protection.

In the following story a desperate pilot and his passenger prepare for the worst when an unseen "pilot" shows up.

Invisible Pilot

During my early forties, I had a private pilot's license and owned a French two-seater airplane known as a taildragger because it needed more care and concentration when taking off and landing.

At the time I shared a private landing strip with a farmer who was also a pilot. We kept both of our planes in his barn. Our landing strip was nothing more than a lane set into the middle of a wheat field. The field was long and narrow, with rows of full-grown trees running parallel to the landing strip. Not much to concern you when you are taking off, but quite daunting when you are making the landing approach.

On this particular day I had brought with me an elderly country neighbor who was about to experience his first flight ever. I flew the old chap around his homestead and other local spots, and then we headed back to the landing strip. I was shocked to see that the wind sock was now indicating a dramatic change of wind direction and strength. In fact, the angle and lift of the windsock made a safe landing look doubtful. I decided to give it a try.

The approach went well until the final seconds. The wind gusted slightly, and I felt the plane veering to the left, where we ended up grazing the wheat. The resulting deceleration was tremendous. With my right hand I reached quickly to close the throttle, and with my left hand I intended to pull back on the stick, which would, I hoped, stop us from cartwheeling tail over nose.

What happened next was quite extraordinary. As I went to push the throttle, I felt a hand come over the top of my own right hand and pull the throttle open to full power. At the same time another foreign hand closed over my left hand and pushed the control stick forward so that the plane went into a nose-down attitude. The result of these control maneuvers was that we broke out of the wheat as if the plane had been catapulted off the deck of an aircraft carrier.

I was in awe of what was happening and had no control of the plane. We shot out of the wheat and headed straight toward the line of trees on the right-hand side. Whoever was in control banked the plane sharply to the left and then leveled it out to start climbing. At about one hundred feet and climbing, on a straight path, I felt the other hands letting go of my own, and I was given back control.

As we gained altitude my first concern was for my passenger, yet he was unfazed by the experience. "That's all right," he said. "It were quite thrillin'."

—Ronald Bisset

The angel's presence filled both passengers with an unusual calm in the midst of a crisis. As the elderly passenger said, "It were quite thrillin'!"

3

Angels Bring Comfort

> Praise be to the God and Father of our Lord
> Jesus Christ, the Father of compassion and the
> God of all comfort, who comforts us in all our
> troubles.
>
> 2 Corinthians 1:3–4

Angels are assigned by God to strengthen, encourage and give comfort when needed. Without their loving presence, many of us would be without hope when we go through the dark night of the soul. Their compassion and comforting presence ward off the deep sense of being alone and unloved. When others fail to be there at the times we most need them, angels fill the void with the love that only God can give.

Many of the angel stories I have been blessed to hear contain this same theme: Someone is rejected, alone, misunderstood, fearful, grieving or abandoned. These are all familiar to our human condition. In the midst of pain and desolation, the Father in His great love for us sends His angels to give us comfort, peace and strength.

Sarah, experiencing the very real grief, despair and helplessness of loss when her beloved dog dies, is visited by an invisible presence offering comfort and hope.

Grief Enveloped by Comfort

Years ago I lost my beloved dog, Jack, after a long struggle to try to preserve his life. I knew I had to go through the grief of the loss, but I had been so attached to Jack that I felt traumatized by his death. It felt as if a family member had died. Most people did not seem to understand the utter despair I felt. I was actually embarrassed by the extent of my sadness, but he had become a part of my family.

For three days I cried night and day. I needed to get back to work, but I just could not motivate myself. It was the lowest point in my life.

Between sobs I prayed, "It's too much, God. Please help me." At that moment I felt the pain evaporate and my tears stopped abruptly. Then I became aware that I was no longer alone. Looking around my living room, I did not see anything unusual, but I felt deep peace—and I knew without a doubt that I would see Jack again someday in heaven. Why had I never thought of this before? The relief was immediate.

I believe an angel was there with me to ease my suffering and to place this knowledge in my heart. Only God's loving intervention could have lifted my sadness so quickly and completely.

I heard knocking on my back patio door and glanced up to see Ruth, my mother-in-law, holding a bouquet of flowers. It was a welcome, unexpected visit, since she lives ninety minutes away. Her quiet concern for my well-being touched me deeply. I thanked God for giving me eight wonderful years with Jack, and for blessing me with an amazing mother-in-law. I am so grateful to God for these blessings—and for all the special moments He has woven into my life.

—Sarah Doohan

Thomas Aquinas taught in his extensive writings on angels that angels have the ability to enlighten our thoughts—to impart truth to us. In the midst of her sorrow, Sarah was visited by an angel of comfort who revealed a truth to her—that she would see her beloved dog again in heaven.

After a series of devastating family crises, Chandra finds herself depressed, sleepless and exhausted. As many people would, she experiences an emotional meltdown from a broken relationship and a beloved parent being stricken with a devastating disease. Just when she doubts that circumstances can ever improve, God in His great mercy and love sends heaven's holy ones to care for her.

Angel Brings Peace

After 22 years of marriage, I went through a very painful divorce. I was completely devastated and did not know how I was to go on. My son still lived at home, and he was torn up as well. My daughter had already moved out but was facing serious life choices. I was still reeling from the aftershock a year later when my mom contracted ampullary cancer and needed surgery. During the three weeks she was in the hospital, my dad, sister and I took shifts so she would never be alone.

I had become worn down physically and emotionally, so I attended a church where I received prayer. That night, as I was lying in bed, I became aware of large, brilliant angels standing around the walls of my room with outstretched wings. They were so tall their heads touched the ten-foot ceiling. In the past year, I had been tormented by fears and unable to sleep. Yet as I looked at those angels I was not afraid. I felt a peace I had never known. I knew the angels were sent by God to watch over me. I had my first restful night's sleep in over a year.

—Chandra Domich

The great prophet Elijah was encouraged and strengthened by an angel when he fled the assassination ordered by Jezebel, the queen who was methodically killing the prophets of God. Elijah had escaped into the desert, where he felt desperately alone as he feared for his life. To avoid the blazing desert sun, Elijah sat down under a broom tree, a desert shrub that offered a little shade. Then he gave up. He actually prayed to die and then lay down and fell asleep.

All at once an angel touched him and said, "Get up and eat." He looked around, and there by his head was a cake of bread baked over hot coals, and a jar of water. He ate and drank and then lay down again. The angel of the LORD came back a second time and touched him and said, "Get up and eat, for the journey is too much for you." So he got up and ate and drank.

1 Kings 19:5–8

Elijah was strengthened immediately by eating the angel's food, so much so that he was able to travel for many days until he reached a cave where he had an extraordinary encounter with God. To all appearances, Elijah had given up. He had prayed for and accepted death, but God was not finished with him.

An observation I made while working as a psychotherapist in psychiatric hospitals was the amount of time patients spent sleeping, seeking to avoid their painful problems. The hospital actually employed several psychiatric aides who spent their entire working days waking up patients and gently encouraging them to leave their rooms and join the other patients. Many would beg, "Just leave me alone and let me sleep."

For people suffering from depression or extreme discouragement, sleep offers a welcome escape. Even in the Garden of Gethsemane, when Jesus told His disciples He was going to leave them, Scripture says, "He found them asleep, exhausted from sorrow" (Luke 22:45).

Angels come when we are in deep need of God's mercy, grace and forgiveness. These moments in our lives are sacred. They are designed by the Holy Spirit to usher us into the holy presence of God. Only the Holy Spirit can convict our hearts of sin and extend the grace necessary for us to confess and be set free from the weight of our sins.

An Angel Acts as a Confessor

My dad was a very good man, but he was not a Christian.

One autumn, when he was working in the hay-mow on our farm, he lost his footing and fell, break-ing his pelvic bone. Upon his arrival at the hospital, he was placed in a ward of men who were dying of cancer. When I went to visit him there, he shared a story with me about what had happened the previous night.

Sleepless in his hospital bed, my father was sud-denly faced with intense guilt resulting from a life-time of long-standing resentments against people he should have forgiven. He told me he had been crying, which was a rare thing for him. He also said that when he was crying, a nurse came into the ward, shut the door and sat on the edge of his bed. She had heard the crying and asked if he would like to talk to her. He confessed to the nurse everything he was struggling with, and as he did he felt his burdens lift. He was so relieved and happy by the end of their talk that he asked the nurse her name so I could meet her.

When she did not return to the ward for her next shift, he asked me to check with the head nurse to see when she would be back. The head nurse looked at the name my father had written and told me that no one by that name worked there. She then went online to check if perhaps the nurse had been substituted from another floor, but the name was not found any-where in the hospital's system.

I explained my dad's interest in seeing her again, and the head nurse told me she had noticed the night before that the ward door had been closed for about an hour and then was opened again. She was not sure why that had happened, as she did not see anyone come or go out of the room. I tried to explain the situation to my dad, but he seemed confused that her name could not be found.

Following Dad's experience, he was ready to surrender his life to God. I am eternally grateful that God provided His angel to take on the image of a compassionate nurse to meet my dad in his time of need. I know his time of confession with the mysterious nurse opened his heart to accept Christ.

—Peggy Robinson

Peggy's dad, faced with a lifetime of guilt, felt the need to confess his sins, so God sent an angel as a nurse to listen to the secrets of his soul. Being in the presence of a holy angel, whether in human or angelic form, ushers a person into God's holy presence. This dad not only felt his burdens lift, but he found salvation through Jesus Christ.

An angel of comfort in the guise of a caring man appears to Patti to remind her of God's eternal care for her and her family. He also joyfully opens her eyes to the many blessings in her life.

An Angel at Disneyland

Two years ago I was going through a very difficult time in my life. My relationship with my son was completely broken. I lost my job; my future looked hopeless as I slid into depression.

For my birthday, my husband—hoping to cheer me up—took me to Disneyland. It had always been a happy place for me, a place where I could be a kid again and forget my problems. I wore a Happy

Birthday button with my name on it. That evening I was really able to get caught up in the enjoyment of the activities.

A man was standing next to me in the crowd. He was about my age and average looking, but with a sparkle in his eyes. Even though I did not know him, he seemed somehow familiar to me. He said, "Happy birthday, Patti! This is all for you!"

I thought it was an unusual thing to say, so I said, "Oh, you saw my name on my birthday button. Thanks."

He responded, and I remember this clearly, "Oh, I know your name. You and I go *way back*." He chuckled, and then he *disappeared*; he simply was not there. I found the whole interaction rather odd, but it felt good all the same. Later, when I got home, I realized that the man was a messenger from God, maybe even my guardian angel, sent to tell me that all the joy, all the beautiful experiences I had had that day, were for me. I felt so loved and special at that moment, and my depression lifted as a result. I know that God cared enough to send me a special birthday message.

—Patti S.

When the angel disappeared, Patti was filled with childlike wonder—so much so that the depression lifted and never returned.

Clinical depression is a major psychiatric disorder that affects 18 to 20 percent of the population. Currently, clinical depression is the leading cause of disability in North

America. Studies show that suicide is the third leading cause of death among those 15 to 25 years of age. The number one cause for those who do commit suicide in this young population is undiagnosed, untreated depression.

This next story reveals the eternal, unbreakable bond that exists between angels and humans. It also illustrates the despair that many young people experience during their teen years.

The teenager in this following encounter admits to suffering from undiagnosed long-term depression until an angel is sent to bring comfort, hope and healing.

Angel Comforts a Depressed Teen

As a high school senior, I traveled alone and arrived a few hours early to a convent retreat. As I waited in the darkened cafeteria, an old nun came to talk to me. I was in a state of long-term depression (although I was unaware of it at the time) and had a constant feeling of general sadness.

The nun spoke to me briefly, but it seemed like an extended period of time. I can remember no clear message, only real joy being in the presence of someone who felt "good" in an incredibly pure and strong way. She encouraged me and soothed my sadness. When she said it was time for her to leave, I begged her to stay, to keep talking. She smiled and said she had to go talk to someone else—another young person, miles away. She said she had been doing this for *hundreds of years*. And then she left.

The room felt empty when so much good departed, but I am still comforted when I think of how she came to me in one of my darkest hours. I also remember the feeling of awe that came from being in the presence of holiness, something that I wish more people could experience. After doing this for hundreds of years, she was an experienced angel!

—Mary Serino

Time stood still for this young person and the angel who ministered to her—because time does not exist in the eternal Kingdom. When we enter into the realm of the sacred, we usually lose awareness of time and space. The transference of life, joy and peace from an angel occurs on the spiritual level—which then infuses our entire being with life. This young woman needed a transfusion of *life*—of God's light into her sad darkness.

Depression is not allowed in proximity to the light of God. It is no small wonder that she begged the angel to remain with her. The compassionate response of the experienced angel is delightful, giving us a glimpse into angels' tireless ministry to the children of God. This story confirms that angels work on assignment from God. And when the mission is complete, they embrace the next person in need.

A Fearful Boy and His Guardian Angel

When my son, Nathan, was four years old, he had a crippling terror of storms and dogs. His fear was so strong that if a dog came anywhere near us he would try to climb up my body. Likewise, during storms he would tremble, cry and need to be held at the first sign of thunder or lightning.

One night there was a particularly violent thunderstorm. Nathan could not sleep and kept coming to me for reassurance. I finally took him to his bedroom and got in bed with him and held him, but he continued to tremble and cry.

I asked him, "Nathan, do you know that Scripture says you have a guardian angel who is always beholding the face of God, and he sees your face, too? He is assigned to protect you. Let's ask your guardian angel to let you know he is protecting you."

So I prayed, "God, would You let Nathan know he has a guardian angel who is always here to protect him? Would You place an angel at each corner of his bed, surrounding him with protection and peace? Let him know You love him and will care for him."

A few days later Nathan told me an amazing story.

"Remember the storm, Mommy? After you left me angels came and stood beside my bed. And then Jesus came, too."

"Jesus came?" I exclaimed. "What did He look like?"

Nathan answered, "He was really big. He had a sash across His front with a sword in it. He said, 'Do you see these angels by your bed? They are here to protect you. And don't worry—the storm will stop.'"

I was in total awe of his story.

I hugged him and said, "Let's thank God for letting you see Jesus and the angels!" After that night, he never again had a fear of storms.

—Joe Carol Thorp

In this amazing account of angelic protection and comfort, Nathan's eyes were opened to see into the spiritual realm to give him the reassuring awareness, not only of guardian angels, but of Jesus Himself. When Jesus spoke to Nathan, his fears evaporated, dispelled by Jesus and His holy angels. Jesus addresses our fears, continually encouraging us to trust that we are in His constant care.

Protection and Comfort for a Single Mother

My husband passed away unexpectedly one January. Following his death, I had undiagnosed medical issues for two years. It was cause for concern, but I had a family to take care of. My children were then sixteen and seventeen, and they were still adjusting to life without their father.

Almost exactly two years after his passing I was in church. The service was almost over, and as I stood to sing the last hymn, I began to hemorrhage. The bleeding went on for two days. When I went to the doctor, she slated me immediately for an emergency hysterectomy. All this, and it was almost Christmas.

Following the surgery I arrived home from the hospital on Christmas Eve. As I walked through the front door, I was met with a surprise. The Christmas tree was up, music was playing, fires welcomed me in both fireplaces and decorations were hung. What a beautiful homecoming! My children were the smiling saviors of Christmas, and I was overjoyed to be back home.

By the time we sat down for supper, however, the temperature outside had plummeted, and our un-heated little beach cottage was starting to feel like an icebox. A few hours later, both children started coming down with stomach flu—complete with fever, chills and intestinal maladies.

We were a pretty pitiful crew at that point. There was not much left to do but crawl into our beds under several blankets. I was distraught and a little frightened by how the day had turned out. What was happening to my family? My prayer was, "Please, Jesus, see us through this trouble." After this simple prayer, I was somehow able to fall asleep.

After sleeping for several hours, I woke for no apparent reason. Opening my eyes, I realized that there was someone—an unknown presence—at the foot of my bed. There, standing in total stillness, was a short, rotund woman. Her hair was pulled back into a bun, and she was wearing a long white gown. She smiled in such a sweet way that I was no longer afraid.

I looked toward my windows to see if there was a reflection that would cause an optical illusion to explain this, but there was not. She started walking along the side of my bed, and as she did, she simply disappeared! As I stared into the darkness where she had just been, the song "Angels Hovering Round Me, Lord" came into my mind. All I could think was, *That was my angel!*

The next morning, as the Christmas dawn brightened our little cottage, I could hear my children milling around the house. When I remembered my angelic visitor who had watched over me, all I could say was, "Thank You, Jesus!"

—B. J. Merrill

Following the loss of her husband, B. J. was carrying the many responsibilities of a single mom coupled with the strain of complicated health problems. Furthermore, all these things happened during the emotionally laden season of Christmas. Feeling increasingly more vulnerable by the moment, she was in need of strength and comfort and cried out to God for help. An angel brought her the strength and comfort she needed to truly celebrate Christmas with her children.

A friend shared with me that she had asthma as a child. Asthma is a frightening disease because the person is not able to breathe normally due to constricted airways in the lungs. Medication is often necessary to open the airways. Unfortunately, my friend's family could not afford the life-saving medicine that was desperately needed. When an asthma attack would strike her as a child, her parents would prop her up in bed with pillows supporting her to enable her to breathe. Her mother would often sit by her bed at night to comfort and pray with her. Since an asthma attack can last a week or two, her mother would become exhausted due to lack of sleep.

One night her mother told her she simply was too tired to stay with her—she had to get some rest. After her mother left the room and when the little girl found herself struggling for breath, she was startled by a large glowing angel who appeared beside her bed. The angel sat down in a rocking chair next to her and began singing the most beautiful, calming lullaby the girl had ever heard. She began to relax, feeling the most incredible peace and comfort she had ever known. Before long, her breathing became normal, and she fell asleep. This same angel visited her on a regular basis during her bouts of asthma. She was always comforted by the peaceful presence during those long nights.

In this next story, Carolyn tells how she is listening to the Bob Dutko radio show while driving to work. Bob is interviewing me about the subject of angels. During the interview, I mention that angels in human form often appear as young men, tall, handsome, with fiery blue eyes, emitting great love, peace and joy. Within a few hours, Carolyn will have an encounter with an angel of God who is sent to lift her anxiety and bring her peace.

A Reassuring Visit

I worked as a cashier at a wholesale club's food court. On slow days I had way too much time to think about my problems. I was under a lot of financial stress and was also concerned about my eldest son, who had strayed from the Lord. One slow day when I was lost in anxious thought, I found myself sliding a tray of food to a customer whom I did not remember ringing up, nor did I remember taking his order. I did not really look at him until that moment, but when I did I saw fiery blue eyes looking back at me. He was very tall and had a beautiful face. I could not look away from his eyes, and I began to smile and feel very happy. He was silent until he turned to leave, saying, "Have a blessed day."

Ever since that day I have felt much better about things in my life. I believe the Lord sent an angel to let me know that my prayers had been heard, and that I need not worry about money or my son, that He would provide solutions for me. I am now closer to the Lord than ever before, and am so much happier.

—Carolyn B.

At the end of a challenging summer speaking schedule, Francis and I were very tired and in need of rest. During the last conference, after being introduced, I was walking slowly up to the podium to teach. Although I was excited by the opportunity to share about God's Kingdom, I was weary physically. When my foot reached the first step, I became aware of an invisible presence on each side of me. Strong hands took hold of both my arms and lifted me up the stairs! An incredible strength flowed into my body from these angelic helpers. Their strong, compassionate presence remained with me until we finished with a healing service later that evening.

At another time, during a healing service, Francis and I were standing at the podium praying for the assembled group. Francis saw a woman in a wheelchair at the front of the church and went down to pray for her. Still at the podium, I was praying with my eyes closed. I felt someone place a hand on my back at the very place where there was pain due to long hours of standing. The hand felt very warm, almost hot, which brought immediate relief to my aching muscles. I assumed it was my husband who had returned to the podium to continue the healing service. When I opened my eyes, no one was there, yet the warm hand was still in place. We were there to minister to God's suffering children, and He sent angels to assist and strengthen us.

Following those two experiences, I had some attendees from those conferences write to me sharing what they had seen. One wrote, "When you walked up the stairs to the podium, there were angels on your right and on your left supporting you," and "when you were praying on the platform, there was a large, luminous angel behind you with his hand on your back." God sent us these descriptions to confirm our experiences with the angels and to remind us that God sends angels to strengthen us when we are weak.

In His lifetime, Jesus experienced the spiritual, emotional and physical demands of ministry. Without a doubt, angels surrounded Jesus in His earthly ministry, bringing Him strength, comfort and companionship.

In the following account Ren is given assurance before her surgery that angels are with her. Yet she still has difficulty letting go of her fears.

Angel Brings Peace to a Fearful Patient

A few months before discovering that I needed surgery, God gave me a vision. With a wave of His hand, I saw Jesus give me two guardian angels. They looked like beautiful people—a man and a woman—with no wings. They wore tightly fitted uniforms, as if the outfits were part of them.

When the time came for my surgery, I was struck with fear. As a nurse worked busily around me, I tried to convince myself that I should be calm, that God was with me. Yet I was under grave spiritual attack.

A man walked into my room, pulled up a chair and sat by my hospital bed. I did not recognize him, yet I felt that I knew him. A wave of fear about the surgery rushed over me, so I turned away from him. Gently, he picked up my hand and began to stroke it. "I am going to take care of you. You are going to be fine," he spoke as he gently held my hand.

Despite his efforts to comfort me, I felt beyond reassurance, so I turned away from him again.

Seeing this, he gently placed my hand by my side and walked over to the nurse. He spoke quietly in her ear, then left.

Seconds later the nurse came over and said, "I'm going to give you a little something to relax you." As she proceeded to prep me, I asked about the doctor who was just here.

The nurse smiled warmly. "There was no one here."

Then I realized he was not a doctor—he was my angel! Thank You, Jesus!

—Ren Brim

When Ren could not receive the comfort of the angel by her bedside, he then turned his attention to the nurse to encourage her to give Ren medicine to calm her down. I wonder how many times an angel is with us during difficult times when we are presented with a choice—to focus on the problem or on God's provision.

The cares and worries of this life can exhaust our emotional, spiritual and physical resources. An angel of God may then be sent to whisper encouragement, filling our entire being with the light of heaven. The angel imparts strength, transforming us so we can face life—not alone, but surrounded by these magnificent heavenly companions.

Dark Night of the Soul

I was in the midst of a dark night of the soul. My marriage was unraveling, and the only place I could find any solace was in my faith. All through the day I alternated between tears and prayers, asking the Lord for help. That night I was too upset to share a room with my husband, so I went to the couch to try to sleep.

I was suffering feelings of helplessness while painful thoughts continued to haunt me. In the darkness of the room where we had spent so much of our life together, the good memories were eclipsed by anxiety. I said a few prayers, hoping for a miracle.

A noise made me open my eyes. When I peered out into the darkness I saw, for the first time in my life, an angel. He was about eight feet tall with bronze skin, and his robe was the same color. He was remarkably beautiful, with large dark eyes and features that somehow combined masculine and feminine traits into a visage that I can only describe as heavenly. Serious yet calm, he seemed to be concentrating all of his power toward me, staring intently at my face while extending one of his hands to my shoulder in a gesture of comfort.

I felt a sense of great compassion, and also one of tremendous peace. The angel stood there for a long time. All the while he kept his arm extended over me, as if he was praying for and protecting me in my state of distress. I began to feel a profound calm throughout my entire being. I knew that everything would be all right, and that I could go back to my bed.

As I rose from the couch, I became aware of another presence, only this one was evil. Peering through the darkness, its mouth twisted with mocking laughter, was a hideous, stark white face. As this thing leered at me with palpable hatred, I turned back to the angel. I could sense his unwavering strength and calm, and I was not afraid. Returning to bed, I fell into a deep sleep.

I will never forget the gentle, compassionate and loving expression on the angel's face. I know he was a messenger from God. The message was one of pure love, and the peace I felt in this being's presence was unlike anything I have known. I believe that this angel has always been with me, and sometimes, in times of trouble, I gain strength by remembering that he is by my side.

—Alli Lopez

Angels have an exceptional capacity to communicate tremendous love and strength without uttering words. Their love and power touch the deepest levels of our being with God's own compassionate care. They can transform any situation in an instant by their appearance—and that experience remains in our hearts forever.

4

Messenger Angels

The smoke of the incense, together with the
prayers of the saints, went up before God from
the angel's hand.

Revelation 8:4

Gabriel is the name of the mighty archangel who stands "in
the presence of God" (Luke 1:19). His name means "mighty
one of God" or "God is my strength." This powerful angel
is God's chief messenger, overseeing and commanding innumerable messenger angels. The Hebrew and Greek words
for angel—*m'aL'akh* and *angelos*—translate to "messenger." These messenger angels under Gabriel's direction act
as intermediaries between God and humans. They carry our
prayers to God (see Revelation 8:3–4), reveal God's will to
us and warn us of impending danger.

Gabriel is named in four separate events in the Bible,
and in each visitation, he delivered an important message

to someone. Gabriel's first two recorded appearances were to Daniel, who received understanding about visions from God concerning Israel's future (see Daniel 8:15–16; 9:21).

Gabriel also appeared to Zechariah, the soon-to-be father of John the Baptist (see Luke 1:19), and to Mary, the mother of Jesus (see Luke 1:26–27). In each appearance, Gabriel brought good news concerning a future event—the greatest being the birth of the Messiah, an event that forever changed the course of humanity.

In this chapter we see that angels continue to deliver messages from God to aid and direct us on our spiritual journeys. And sometimes, as we will also see, they offer assistance, insight and even provision.

Jesus—The Divine Physician

My husband, Rob, became gravely ill with a blood disorder, causing massive internal bleeding. His spleen was so enlarged with blood that it weighed eight pounds. After he had gone through numerous hospital visits and fifty blood transfusions, the doctors told us they had done everything they could. They sent us home with a death sentence. We were devastated by the news, but we somehow held on to hope and our faith in Jesus grew stronger.

One evening a friend called with the name of a surgeon who was testing new procedures. When we met the doctor, he was positive he could help my husband. We booked surgery for the next week. I was overjoyed at this new hope, but fear was making a home in my heart. The procedure was new, so I was still afraid of losing my husband.

Alone in church the next day, I knelt to pray for Rob. As I poured out my heart, a small man walked quickly up the aisle, looked intently into my eyes and asked, "Do you believe in miracles?"

"Yes," I replied. After introducing himself as Paul, he proceeded to tell me that his son had been healed by a doctor.

He declared, "Jesus is the Divine Physician, but sometimes He uses doctors to heal us." Then Paul prayed the following prayer with me: "Lord Jesus, I don't know why this young lady is here. Maybe she is praying for someone who is ill, or maybe she likes spending time with You. I ask You, Lord, to bless her with Your peace, joy and love." After finishing his prayer, Paul looked at me and said, "Always count your blessings." I was filled with peace about the upcoming surgery.

Ten hours of surgery and fourteen units of blood later, my husband survived. I believe the Divine Physician guided the surgeon's hands that day. Paul, too, was the divine breath of God blowing new hope into my spirit in that church. Praise God for His holy angels!

—Anita Guariglia

Some Christians do not believe that God uses doctors, surgery, medication and countless other specialists to bring healing to our bodies and minds. When Rob experienced a life-threatening medical emergency, however, God sent an angel of hope to Anita, to assure her that Jesus, the Divine Physician, was sending a miracle through the hands of a skilled surgeon. "Do not forget to entertain strangers," Scripture says, "for by so doing some people have entertained angels without knowing it" (Hebrews 13:2).

When Andre is assigned a dangerous task, prayer brings life-saving changes in a police patrol's actions through an angelic encounter.

Death by Hit Squad Averted

I was an officer for 21 years in the South African Police Service, where I was a member of the Unrest and Violent Crimes Unit tasked with tracking down and apprehending violent suspects. We relied on a large network of informants to trace wanted criminals. In some cases informers were double agents working with the police and criminals at the same time.

One Christmas morning, my team and I were placed on standby in an effort to apprehend a violent gang of hit-squad members. Hit squads were generally made up of ruthless ex-military men who were willing to carry out murder for whoever would pay the most.

We received a call from an informant who gave us details about where the suspects would be found, and my team assembled to go over our operational planning. We would be going in an unmarked vehicle, and I was to drive. Marked uniform vehicles were to be used as backup for our operation.

On the way to the target area, I remember praying as we drew closer. I felt as though someone was urging me to diverge from the planned route to our destination and go a different way. I ignored this and drove on, but before long it returned, stronger than before. I felt unsure and slightly confused about what was happening. I continued on the planned route, but the feeling intensified. It felt so real that I was overwhelmed and finally informed my team that we were going to take an alternate route that would let us approach the complex from the rear instead of the front.

When we got close enough to the target area to view the complex, we could see the hit-squad members waiting by their vehicle with the doors open, watching the road going toward the front of the complex—the road that we would have been on had I not changed our course. We were able to catch them off guard, before they were able to reach their AK-47s loaded with bullets that were intended to tear us apart.

A one-sided gun battle ensued, and we were able to apprehend all of them without a single shot being fired at my team. I believe it was my guardian angel who was warning me of the imminent danger that awaited us. Since that day I have been in numerous life-threatening situations, and whenever I get an uneasy feeling I now know to listen to it. The angels have never led me astray.

—Andre van Aswegen

Andre received three "urges" to change the route for their mission, each one more urgent than the last. The final one was overwhelming. We can be thankful that angels do not fail to carry out their assignments.

As humans, we share an innate desire for a deep connection with the living God. We find ourselves groping for answers and for guidance in the complex issues of life.

91

The majority of people who came to see me for counseling when I was in private practice were seeking direction about major life decisions. During these stressful times of emotional upheaval, we seek the voice of reason and wisdom that will point us in the right direction. After years of listening to individuals and families, I have come to the conclusion that during these times of transition God often seems distant and unavailable to many Christians.

In the confusing maze of our spiritual journeys, therefore, we seek a mediator—someone to deliver God's message to us or to help us understand what He is saying. Historically this is true. When Moses ascended Mount Sinai in the desert on behalf of the children of Israel, he would listen to Yahweh and then convey God's will to the people. Like those wandering souls, we typically lose belief in our ability to hear God or to discern the signs He is giving us.

When we cannot seem to hear His voice we turn to priests, ministers, rabbis or spiritual directors to speak on God's behalf as Moses did. There is absolutely nothing wrong with this proven approach during a life crisis when we are overwhelmed by extreme difficulties—at those times when our lives are collapsing around us. The still, small voice within us can be silenced by the voices of fear engulfing us.

Perhaps you are struggling with a difficult marriage, medical treatment options, fear about a wayward son or daughter, a career decision, financial difficulties or God's will concerning the future. In addition to wise counselors, God has provided messenger angels to bring wisdom to those seeking guidance in making crucial life decisions. Often, as we pray, an angel delivers God's guidance directly to us as we wait in prayerful silence. The confusion and fear fade away as the angel conveys God's love and peace.

Much intercessory prayer surrounds the following story of a man desperately in need of an intervention from God.

An Angel Posing as a Friend

I was working on the manuscript for a new book with the help of a retired man from our church who had offered to do some editing. He was doing excellent work, and I was finally beginning to settle into a steady work flow. My daughter, who had recently gone back to college, called to ask if I would stay with her kids for a week at the start of her spring semester. Her farm is about seventy miles from my home, too far to commute, so I prepared plenty of work for John—the man who was helping me—to look over while I was away.

The Sunday before I was to leave for my daughter's home, our pastor announced in church that John was in the hospital. He was very ill and needed our prayers. I called our pastor the next morning to see how John was doing.

"Not very well," Pastor Steve told me.

"Do you mean he might not make it?" I asked.

"That's a real possibility," he said somberly.

I was devastated—both out of concern for John as well as for fear that I might lose my editor. Many of my poems have to do with alcohol or its effects on the family. John had told me as we were working that his dad was an alcoholic and that he and his brothers had been given away to a family that was extremely strict with them.

John is the typical oldest son in an alcoholic family. Hardworking, high achieving, *magna cum laude* from Harvard—I was afraid he had the same program running through his neural computer as I did: "Why try? Life is too painful." With this in mind, I prayed for him quite a bit while I looked after my grandchildren.

One night I awoke at the farm and could not get John off my mind. As I began to pray for him, I pictured Jesus on the throne in heaven. I saw myself take John's hand as I led him up to the throne, where we both knelt at Christ's feet. I told Jesus about my fear for John, although I cannot remember exactly what I said. I eventually fell asleep, feeling somewhat reassured about John's situation.

A few days later, as I arrived home from the farm, the phone rang. It was John's wife, whom I scarcely knew. She said, "My daughter and I want to thank you for talking John into going into treatment for alcoholism."

I said, "I haven't spoken to John. I've been at my daughter's all week. I had no idea John was an alcoholic."

In a perplexed tone, she said, "Well, he told us that you came to the hospital and talked him into going into treatment. He's going as soon as they discharge him." That was the easiest intervention for alcoholism that I never did!

—Mary Soergel

The heart of this story is God's redeeming love in John's life—a soul literally sinking into the arms of death was rescued by an angel disguised as a friend. Mary reached for

John's hand during prayer and led him to the source of life. In that moment, God sent a messenger angel to bring His child the encouragement and strength necessary to seek treatment for alcoholism.

Thomas Aquinas said we are like children who stand in need of masters to enlighten us and direct us; and God has provided for this by appointing His angels to be our teachers and guides. Our early mothers and fathers in the faith accepted the intervention of angels in their daily lives. They understood the importance of listening for God's wisdom that angels impart. A word of caution: It is important to understand that angels convey only God's messages. If we encounter an angelic messenger sent by God with a message from Him, the angel will speak of God's loving care and provision. As with every spiritual experience, God is at the center. Angels reaffirm God's caring involvement in the midst of our earthly journeys.

One of the highlights of the next story is the lovely way the Lord answers the desire of Christa's heart to have an angelic encounter.

An Angel in Overalls

When I became a believer, a Christian friend told me of her encounters with an angel in human form. Inspired by her stories, I prayed a simple prayer, "Lord, please allow me to meet an angel one day."

A few weeks later as I was walking into a grocery store, I heard these words clearly: *You will meet an angel today.*

I chuckled, rolled my eyes and thought, *Wow, wouldn't that be great.*

After buying my groceries I was pushing my cart to the exit when I saw a bearded, white-haired man in denim overalls leaning against the wall by the door. His smile was very pleasant, and he kept looking at me with considerable intensity.

A woman pushing her cart in front of me gave me an odd look when I greeted him. As I drew closer to him, he said, "You have yourself a good night."

"Thank you. You, too," I replied. Again, the woman gave me a puzzled look. I smiled at her, but was confused by her behavior. The old man followed me out of the store but turned the other way as I walked to my car. Within seconds, I glanced back and he was gone. He had vanished into thin air; he could not possibly have walked out of sight in the parking lot in those few seconds.

Then I realized why the woman had looked at me so strangely. She could not see the man: He was an angel. I knew that God had answered my prayer. What a wonderful God we serve, that He would care about even the smallest requests we bring to Him!

—Christa Sarazen

Obviously, Christa was the only one in the store who could see the angel—who vanished after blessing her. This proved to her that God cares about the smallest requests we bring to Him.

The following story was shared with me by a good friend who is also involved in the healing ministry. This encounter reveals the daily care we receive from these beings of light.

Guidance for a Priest

For nearly three decades, much of my ministry has been on the road, conducting healing missions and teaching conferences. Early on in this work, God gave me several boosts to my faith. Most of these were the miraculous healings I was privileged to witness, but one involved an angel.

I had finished ministering at a church rather late one night but did not have a place to sleep in the area. My plan was to leave the church and drive to the home of the rector at whose church I would be ministering the next day. I ate some supper, packed my few things and started off toward my next destination.

The drive was going well until, somewhere in rural New Jersey, I got lost. No matter how hard I tried, I could not find any of the major roads that my map showed, nor had there been any gas stations for many miles. In my helplessness, I asked God for help.

Within a few minutes, I saw in my rearview mirror the flashing lights of a police car. He was pulling me over. I thought, *I wasn't speeding. I didn't run a stop sign. What is this?*

The police officer walked up to my window and said, "Father, if you go one mile ahead, turn left, go a half mile, and turn left again, you'll come to the New Jersey Turnpike."

I thanked him, and as he was returning to his police car, a cold chill went up my spine. I thought to myself, *I changed out of my clerical attire after the service, and now I'm wearing sports clothes. How did he know to call me "Father"? And how does he know where I need to go?*

This angelic visitation gave a renewed strength to my faith. Needless to say, I really trusted God to bring healing at the next night's service—and He did.

—The Reverend Canon Dr. Mark A. Pearson

Being lost is something most of us can relate to. How many times does insecurity creep into our minds when we have no idea where we are or how to get to where we need to be—especially late at night on a darkened road in a rural area?

A Cold, Moonless Night

I was single, twenty years old, and on my way home from a convention in downtown Detroit. Although I worked downtown, I always took surface roads to and from my parents' home in the northwest part of the city. That night, however, I thought it might be safer to drive on the freeway where I would not have to stop every few blocks. I was unfamiliar with the freeway system, but there were signs. *How hard could it be?* I thought and started out on this new route.

After taking what I thought were the exits to get to my parents' house, I ended up on a deserted country road in a northeast suburb of Detroit, where I ran out of gas. It was a cold, moonless night in November, and the only structure I could see was the outline of a house up the road. I walked toward the unlit house, hoping that someone would be there to help me.

With some trepidation I rang the doorbell, knocked and finally pounded my fist on the door. No answer. As I looked around the area, I realized that this house and all the other houses around it were abandoned. Apparently, I had driven onto a proposed extension to the freeway system, and these houses were awaiting demolition. I was miles away from a phone and help, desperate and fully aware of my vulnerability.

I went back to my car, got in and started to cry. Feeling very frightened and alone, I prayed, "God, if You're real, I need help!"

At that moment, an old car with two elderly men inside pulled up alongside me. One of the men asked if I needed help. Crying and unable to hide my distress, I nodded yes. The man got out and motioned for me to get into the backseat of their two-door sedan. I hesitated but decided it was my only option.

After traveling several miles, we reached a gas station, where we filled a gas can. Afterward, they drove me back to my car. They knew exactly what to do; they opened the hood, took the air cleaner off and poured some of the gas into the carburetor. Then they poured the rest of the gas into the tank. All this time, none of us spoke a word.

I slid into my car eager to get started when I realized I had forgotten to say thank you. I looked around, but the car was gone. It had been only a few seconds—but there was no sign of anyone, anywhere. The road was, once again, dark and deserted. The truth, however, is that I had never really been alone.

—Marieanne Rose

As we have seen, when angels appear in human form to bring us the assistance we need, they usually disappear in an instant. Faith does not seem to be a prerequisite for angelic help. In the preceding story, Marieanne prayed, "God, if You're real, I need help!" Fortunately for us, God does not ask if we believe in Him before He sends help.

God hears every cry of the human heart. When Jesus stood at the tomb of His friend Lazarus, who had been dead for four days, He looked up and said, "Father, I thank you that you have heard me" (John 11:41). Jesus then called Lazarus back from the dead. Jesus had complete confidence that when He prayed, God heard His prayers.

Jane's prayers for her children are heard by God, and He sends an angel in human form to give her the message of how to pray for their salvation.

A Mother's Prayer

Years ago while riding a bus to Connecticut to be with my mom, who had just buried her sister, I began thinking of my seven children. I thought of their relationships with God, and asked God in my heart what more I could do to help them.

After returning home to Vermont, I was attending a weekly prayer meeting. While the meeting was going on, there was a knock at the door. The group leader was busy, so I opened the door to find a short woman with a rather large suitcase who said she was looking for the bus depot. I said I would drive her there after the prayer meeting, so she joined us.

When the meeting ended, the woman approached me, took my hand and said, "God has a message for you. He wants you to pray for their minds to be prepared and opened to receive His Word." She then repeated the message. I remembered the question I had asked the Lord while on the bus. I had not told anyone about this question.

When I think about this unusual encounter, I just smile, because I now know that I was visited by an angel. I have never forgotten her message and have prayed her words—not only for my children but for others as well, that their minds be prepared and opened to receive God's Word.

—Jane Hennessey

One day I received the following "Dear Judith" letter:

A Supernatural Encounter

My birthday was April 5, and it was not a good one. My husband and I were attending a friend's wedding reception, but I became very ill and had to return home. I was so disappointed!

The next day at the grocery store, I was pushing the cart to my car. I noticed a nice-looking, clean-cut man walking toward me. He looked to be middle-aged and wore khaki pants and a short-sleeved pastel plaid shirt. He was holding a bouquet of flowers.

The man passed in front of me and our eyes locked. I remember that his eyes were peaceful and loving. I fumbled for words. All I could think to say was, "Someone is going to love those."

"These are for you," he said in a quiet, gentle voice. He then handed me the beautiful bouquet, which was made up of the prettiest flowers from the store, including Gerbera daisies, one of my favorites.

The man had such a kind demeanor that it somehow did not seem awkward for a stranger to give me flowers. I felt surprised, joyful—and very peaceful. I squeaked out a "Thank you" to the smiling stranger before he quietly walked away. I called out, "Thank you so much. I just had my birthday!" He glanced back, smiled and kept walking.

My experience became clear: I had seen an angel. God had answered my prayers. He had responded to the desire of my heart. Not only had the Lord given me a birthday present via His messenger, He had redeemed the disappointing birthday.

Even now I tear up with joy when I think of what happened that day. I will never forget the man's eyes and the supernatural love that radiated from them, which still touches my spirit even through the memory. I have no doubt that God lovingly sent His servant to bless me for my birthday.

—Andi Smith

During difficult times in our lives we sometimes feel overwhelmed by the stress and suffering we have to endure. Our usual coping skills seem to stop working. As darkness engulfs Lana, an unusual passenger joins her on a flight to Paris.

Angel at Thirty Thousand Feet

About fifteen years ago, I was going through a very dark time in my life and began to spiral downward. My husband and I were going through a rough

patch, my youngest son had cancer and I was struggling at work. In addition, several family members had recently died, so funerals were becoming
commonplace.

When I hit my lowest point, I could not eat; my
weight began to plummet. I had lost my desire to
live.

My husband and I worked for an airline that had
just opened a new route to Paris. He thought it might
help me if we took the flight simply to get away. After
we arrived at the airport, the agent told us that the
flight was full. We were flying as "non-revs," which
meant that we could have seats only if they were not
all booked by passengers. Actually, I was relieved. But
as we were leaving, the agent came running to us and
said two seats had just become available. We rushed
on board as the doors were about to close.

After my husband drifted off to sleep, the nicely
dressed Middle Eastern man sitting next to me began
talking. For some reason I opened up to him about
the deep sadness I was feeling, which was mainly
about my son. Reaching under his seat, he produced
a Bible and started to read passages that spoke to my
heart. We talked for almost seven hours. I did not
think to question at the time that he knew the names
of our two sons. He advised me never to doubt the
power of a mother's prayer for her children and encouraged me never to give up.

What he said next made my heart skip a beat:
"Lana, I was not supposed to be on this flight." He
then reached into his pocket and handed me his plane
ticket and said, "Please, Lana dear, read the flight

number on this ticket." I was stunned to see that not only was it not the right flight, but it was the wrong seat and even the wrong day. He smiled, looked at me with loving eyes and said, "My dear Lana, God loves you beyond words that you could understand. Now do you know why I am here?"

"Are you here for me?" I asked.

"I am here for you," he replied. "Please remember that God loves you, and that you must live."

When we landed, he gave me a hug and walked away. I knew in that moment that I had been brought back to life. I had regained the will to live.

—Lana Kelley

Lana reports joyfully that after sharing her worries with the "Middle Eastern man," she found the will to live again. How interesting that God provided two seats at the final boarding call! In addition, the angel knew the names of her two sons—and the Scriptures that would feed her soul. He called her to life, which is the message of hope that God always speaks through His messenger angels.

In the following story, Tara, a young wife and mother, receives bad news. Struggling with an intense sense of loneliness in the hospital, she discovers a supernatural presence.

Supernatural Presence During a Lonely Night

During one long winter, I had suffered from a string of illnesses, mostly colds and various strains of the flu. After months of sickness I was physically depleted. By now, however, I had a job with benefits, so I was able to make a doctor's appointment.

After my appointment, the doctor sent me to the hospital ER for X rays and blood work. This made me nervous, so I asked my husband to join me. I had been in the ER most of the day and was ready to go home to my precious four-year-old.

As I was leaving, the doctor asked that we wait for the blood results, as the X rays were normal. She explained that if I had pneumonia, I might need to be admitted. I decided to send my husband home while I waited for the results.

The doctor returned, accompanied by another doctor. I could tell from their expressions that they had bad news. They told me that the blood work showed that I had leukemia! They assured me that the diagnosis was accurate.

After a CAT scan, I was taken to a private room, where I waited for the oncologist to explain treatment options. Overwhelmed with anxious thoughts, I realized, *I'm all alone.* At that moment, a warm and radiant glow began to manifest over my right shoulder. Even though my parents are in heaven, I became aware of their loving presence. Along with my parents, I sensed a much greater presence that enveloped me in comforting warmth and light. Someone took my right hand and squeezed it gently, conveying to me, *You are not alone.* I felt a loving, gentle reassurance as if someone were saying, "We are all here with you, and we love you!" I knew it was Jesus and His angels.

Every time I tell this story I cry. I felt strengthened and knew that my future was in His loving care—I would be okay. God's angels were with me, ministering throughout a day that marked the beginning of my personal relationship with Jesus. Less than a decade has passed since that life-changing day. I pray that no matter what you are facing, you will know that Jesus is always with you.

—Tara LaPlante

Throughout that long day, Tara encountered kind, unusually helpful people, right up to the moment in the hospital room, where she was comforted by Jesus Himself. Heaven surrounded her as a warm, radiant light enveloped her, and Jesus held her hand and gave her a message that is for all of us: "You are not alone."

5

Angels Encourage Worship

"A time is coming and has now come when the
true worshipers will worship the Father in spirit
and truth, for they are the kind of worshipers the
Father seeks. God is spirit, and his worshipers
must worship in spirit and in truth."

John 4:23–24

After Lynne and I moved to Jerusalem, the Holy Spirit
began to prompt us to go deeper in our prayer lives. We
were both very zealous for God but fairly immature in our
understanding of His Kingdom. All that began to change
when we attended a prayer meeting hosted by an American
evangelist visiting Israel.

My mentor and spiritual mother, Ms. Floride Ameil, had
lived and worked for God in Jerusalem for fifty years, having
moved there from South Carolina as a young woman to serve
the Lord. Floride was a woman of remarkable faith and had

taken Lynne and me under her wing to mentor us. Floride insisted that we attend a meeting that evening for Christians who were living and working in Israel. After offering many excuses not to attend, we found ourselves following Floride to the Church of St. Peter in Gallicantu (meaning "Cock's Crow"), the church built over the site where Peter had denied Jesus on the night of our Lord's passion.

When we entered the church, the worship had already started and several people danced past us with radiant faces, expressing great joy. Most of the people in attendance were fully engaged in wonder and praise. Neither Lynne nor I had ever seen anyone move around during a church service, much less dance! *Uncomfortable* would not begin to describe how we felt. Not knowing how to respond, we proceeded to go to the very back row of the church and knelt down to pray.

In retrospect, I realize how out of place we must have looked. Everyone else was dancing, including Floride, who was in her seventies. And there we were, hiding in the back pew. When the evangelist asked us to come to the front for prayer, we balked. Floride again insisted, so we went forward but slipped to the back of the line, not expecting anything to happen.

After the prayer I returned to my safe back pew. The worship continued with great joy. The entire group was thanking God for the ways He had touched them. Many were healed of various sicknesses; some experienced deep inner healing and freedom from long-held bondages. I tried to enter into their celebration of God's goodness, but I failed.

Praying silently, I heard a quiet but authoritative voice within me that said simply, *Praise Me.* I tried to ignore it, but a second time the voice came, only more adamant: *Praise Me.* I began to look around to see if someone was behind me. (Of course no one was there since I was in the back pew.) I heard the voice again, except this time it was more demanding. I realized with much sadness that I had never truly worshiped my Father God, and worse, I did not know how. How does one abandon oneself totally, focusing one's entire being on Him? I definitely needed help. I wanted desperately to be obedient, but how?

I began by saying out loud (slowly and quietly at first), "I praise You." I repeated this for several minutes wondering if this would be acceptable, aware that I was still inside my own thoughts and performing as usual. My childhood church regularly sang three hymns before the sermon and one in closing, and that was all. I had no frame of reference for praising Him. What a sad realization that was!

As I continued to try my best, I became aware of someone unseen who began gently to lift my arms over my head in a posture of praise and surrender. My arms felt as light as a feather and remained up without any effort on my part. I was astonished at the strong, peaceful presence that was all around me. This feeling permeated my entire being. I prayed that this moment would never end. Now that I was focused on adoring Jesus, everything else faded away. I wondered, *Is this sensation similar to the experiences that mystics and saints have shared for centuries? Bliss!*

Then without warning, my language changed from English to a beautiful, exotic-sounding new language, one that seemed filled with thanksgiving, praise and passion. I had no previous experience with any of this, but knew in my deepest heart that this was a heavenly language spoken by the Holy Spirit to my Father in heaven.

You would think I might have accepted the entire experience as the answer to my heartfelt prayers for intimacy.

Instead, I lacked the courage to remain there. Years of skepticism kicked in, and I withdrew from the experience with Him. I allowed fear to make me retreat into my safe, comfortable space. Instantly my decision turned His presence away from me, and I became aware of the heaviness of my arms that were still extended to Him. They now felt as if they had weights attached to them. I was devastated! How could I have turned away from that dazzling presence? How could I have said no? I tried to return to the experience, but it was too late. The moment had passed.

I wept unashamedly and was inconsolable on the walk home through the Old City of Jerusalem back to the Convent of Ecce Homo, where Lynne and I rented rooms. After our evening prayer, she returned to her room for the night. I slipped out of bed, kneeling on the cold stone floor, and begged God to forgive me and to come again and give me a second chance. Several hours later I drifted off into a fitful sleep, utterly disappointed in myself.

Around three a.m. I was awakened by a radiant light. A holy presence filled my room. Love permeated the air. My arms were lifted again by unseen hands, only this time a heavenly language erupted from my mouth in song. I had never heard anything like this song. It was perfect in every way. I knew it was a song of divine longing and adoration for my Lord, and it was somehow being returned to me by Him. Every place within me, my entire being—body, mind and spirit—was flooded and saturated with that love. An indescribable, ecstatic joy filled me. I was deeply thankful that He had given me a second chance.

That incredible experience forever changed the way I think about worship. Did God need me to praise Him? No. But He showed me that I needed to praise and worship Him in order to enter into His sacred presence and then receive all He has to offer. When some of the Pharisees told Jesus to make the people stop praising Him as He rode into Jerusalem on the day we now call Palm Sunday, His response was that even the stones would cry out if He tried to stop the people from praising Him (see Luke 19:39–40). God does not need our praise, but we need to enter through the door of worship if we want to abide with Him.

The seraphim, cherubim and thrones praise God constantly in heaven. These worshiping angels want us to share in the joy and love they experience. I believe that angels were all around me that night in the church, lifting my arms, encouraging me, showing me the way to my Father's heartfelt love.

A remarkable number of people have shared their experiences with angels during times of worship. God inhabits the praises of His people (see Psalm 22:3), and the angels join us in praising Him.

Angels Join Worship

One time I was in the basement of a home with my high school youth group during a spontaneous worship gathering. We sang several songs, but the song "I Exalt Thee" seemed to have a special attraction for our hearts and invited us into the Lord's presence. We must have been singing for about half an hour, repeating the chorus with our eyes closed. The adults were all upstairs finishing their dinners and visiting together. We thought they must have come downstairs and joined us when the volume and perceived number of voices increased remarkably. All of us opened our eyes at the same time, expecting to

see the adults standing there with us, but they were
just coming down the steps to check on us. They had
heard more voices singing than we had started with
and thought other kids had joined us.

—Robin Morrison

This theme of increased volume is attributed to angelic
worship. Since one of the primary functions of angels is to
worship God, they enter into human worship when possible.
Often we simply hear them, but occasionally they become
visible to the assembly, as in the following story.

Singing with Angels

One Sunday, when I was singing in the choir at
Holy Nativity Church, we were preparing to sing
an anthem that was very challenging. When the or-
ganist started playing the introduction, angels appeared, joining the choir and praising God. When
we sang, there were notes being sung that were not
even written into the music! It was absolutely glorious. There were 24 angels, dressed in white robes,
singing with us. When the service was over, I asked
the person sitting next to me if she had heard or
seen the angels. Wide-eyed and with excitement,
she said yes. This serves as a reminder of the words
of Jesus from Matthew 18:20: "Where two or three
come together in my name, there am I with them."
Heaven can join, whether the congregation is small
or large.

—Judith F. Bradley

The following story is a remarkable account of a committed young couple launching into the mission field to establish a Bible school in the worst part of town, an area plagued by drugs and prostitution. Since they lack a worship leader, God supplies a fully decked-out bagpiper with a message of amazing grace.

Angel Brings Music and Peace

After Bible school training in the U.S., my husband, George, and I were sent into God's mission field in the United Kingdom. Our assignment was to plant and direct a Bible college in Coventry, England.

The ministry had procured a rundown, two-story warehouse in the heart of Coventry that needed a tremendous amount of renovation. This was to be the site of the school. One day, as we were standing in a little storage room looking at some used desks, old chairs and boxes of office supplies, discouragement hit us. Hard. There was no school, no classrooms, and it was up to us to get it started. Students had signed up and we had nowhere to put them. We felt alone and overwhelmed.

School started that fall with a handful of students from around England. Classes began each day at nine a.m. with forty minutes of worship time organized by the students.

One Monday we discovered that no one had signed up to lead worship. George decided we should have quiet devotions instead. After he said the morning prayer, the students fanned out to pray.

At that point, I began to hear someone playing a bagpipe. I stepped over to the windows overlooking the rough, terraced Coventry houses but did not see anyone.

That's, odd, I thought. *What would a bagpiper be doing in this part of town? And what is that song?* As the music grew louder, I recognized the melody, and the familiar words from the eighteenth-century hymn ran through my mind:

> Amazing grace! (how sweet the sound)
> That saved a wretch like me!
> I once was lost, but now am found,
> Was blind, but now I see.

Astounded to have such a poignant reminder of God's love accompanying our devotional time, I began to weep. Later the students told me they felt their burdens lift, hearts lighten and their courage being renewed.

When the bell rang for class, students ran to the windows to see the bagpiper, *but the music stopped* just as we finished our devotions. I ran down the stairs, almost running over Ian, our Scottish ministry director. "Ian," I asked breathlessly, "did you hear the music?"

"Aye!" he said. "I did! I dinna know who he was, but there was a mon standing in the doorway playing a bagpipe. He was dressed in full Highland dress, including Prince Charlie jacket, kilt and everything!"

"Ian, where did he go?" I asked, thinking of Hebrews 13:2: "Do not forget to entertain strangers, for by so doing, some people have entertained angels without knowing it." Since only a few minutes had elapsed, I ran outside the front door to where Ian said the "mon" had been, looking both ways. I could see no one.

I looked up and noticed our sign that read "Charis Bible College." The word *charis* is a Greek word meaning "grace." Indeed, God had sent us a messenger who had played "Amazing Grace," a reminder of the One who was overseeing our ministry. I felt such peace to know that God cared about our school enough to send a bagpiping angel to bless us.

—Krissy Maxwell

Just as some people are graced by God to see angels, others are graced by Him to hear them, as the following intriguing incident suggests.

Angel Tenors Behind Me

I had just been diagnosed with cancer. Since others in our church had recently received bad news, our pastor called us together for a worship service. I was sitting with friends four rows from the back, and we were experiencing a powerful presence of the Lord. I soon became aware of several male tenor voices behind me. I looked to see if I knew them and was shocked to see that no one was there, yet I kept hearing their remarkable voices. The rows behind me were empty. I asked my friend who used to sing in a group called Sweet Adelines if she could hear the voices. With a smile she sighed and said yes. She could not see them either. I believe it was the sound of a heavenly chorus, and it gave me such comfort and joy.

—Kathi Smith

Angels love to come to meetings where people are praising God, and they cannot resist joining us—or is it we who join them? It is within their nature to praise God continuously. Angels are literally drawn to places where God is worshiped.

Kayla, a hospital technician, is directed by the Holy Spirit to pray for healing for an ICU patient. What follows is a powerful and delightful testimony of healing and angelic worship.

A Worshiping Angel Appears

I am a technician at a hospital. One day I was going to take a few X rays with a portable machine in the intensive care unit. As I walked into the room, I felt instantly that God wanted to heal the young patient lying there. He was nearly unconscious and being kept alive by a breathing machine. His girlfriend was in the room, so I asked her if I could pray for him. To my relief, she agreed enthusiastically. A doctor came in, so I had to leave without praying.

When my shift ended, I went to his room. His girlfriend told me that he had been near death due to cancer and infection, but that his doctors had seen steady improvement—enough to plan to take him off the ventilator the next morning.

We stood on each side of his bed and prayed for God to heal him. He nodded in agreement as we prayed. Before leaving, his girlfriend and I exchanged phone numbers. During the night, she sent me a text saying that he was doing so well they had removed the breathing machine. She invited me to visit and pray again.

A week later I was finally free to visit the young man, who had been moved out of the intensive care unit. He shared a remarkable story. He said the night we prayed, he saw not two but three people around his bed. I was at his right, his girlfriend at his left, and there was also a woman standing at the foot of his bed singing gospel songs. He said, "If you knew me, you would know that gospel music is not familiar to me." He said, "I've never had an experience like that before." I believe the singing woman was an angel sent to minister God's love to him.

—Kayla Stewart

Our dear friend Barbara Shlemon, author and speaker, spent more than fifty years in the healing ministry traveling throughout the world. She shared the following story with me.

Angels in Alaska

A Christian worship leader recounted this story about a meeting on a cold, snowy night in Alaska. Outside, the winter moaned and hissed against the frosted church windows. Inside the church, though, people were warm, happy and singing song after song praising God. No one wanted to stop. After one last praise song, the people stopped singing and the musicians put down their instruments, but the singing kept on going! Everyone there heard it. Was this a heavenly choir who got so carried away they did not notice when everyone in the church had stopped?

Next time you are singing praise songs to the Lord, sing with all your heart and then ask God to send His angels to join you.

—Barbara Shlemon

In his book *When He Is Come: An Account of the 1858–60 Revival in Wales* (Evangelical Movement of Wales, 1959), Eifion Evans describes this occurrence:

> An unusual phenomenon in this revival was the "singing in the air" which many reliable witnesses heard. The sound of heavenly angelic voices, sweetly and softly joined in harmony, was overpowering. The effect on the listener was to render him incapable of movement as though nailed to the spot.

"Nailed to the spot"—unable to move in the holy presence of these brilliant angelic beings. Imagine the heavy peace that settled on those participants of that great revival! Similar accounts occur throughout history and have been recorded by people from all walks of life.

At Christian Healing Ministries, several times a year we teach our School of Healing Prayer on our campus. The final day we pray with the students for their personal prayer requests. Following prayers for each person, we lower the lights and allow the students a quiet time to soak in God's loving presence. Occasionally Francis will sing in the Spirit over the class.

Many years ago, the Holy Spirit led Francis to sing in his prayer language over a large group at a Full Gospel Business Men's Fellowship meeting led by Demos Shakarian. It was a regional conference in McCormick Place in Chicago, Illinois. At first Francis was hesitant to sing, not being professionally trained; however, he wanted to be obedient to the guidance of God. He relented and sang a prayer in tongues. When he finished, many of those businessmen were weeping openly as God moved deeply and profoundly within each one.

From that day on, Francis has continued to pray in this way when he feels so directed by the Holy Spirit. The results are always the same: numerous inner healings. Many times when Francis has finished singing a prayer at one of our school sessions, a man's voice with great range and clarity will continue to sing—even after Francis has left the room. We have had this reported far too many times to doubt its credibility.

Following our return to the U.S. after those years in Jerusalem, Lynne and I traveled for a year across the country and then throughout Canada, speaking in churches and home groups about our time in Israel. We wanted to concentrate our energy on alerting Christians to pray for peace in that war-torn country.

One evening we were invited to share with a home prayer group. The people there were almost all young professionals wanting to update their knowledge of the conflict in the Middle East. Before Lynne and I shared with the group, a lovely young woman with a guitar led us in worship. Two observations struck me as I listened to her. First of all, she glowed, literally, while she worshiped God. Secondly, we were not familiar with any of the praise songs she was singing. We had been in Christian fellowship most of our lives, and yet the songs were unfamiliar.

We approached her, introduced ourselves and asked if she had written the songs. Her response startled us. She said she had learned the lyrics from angels in the desert. No doubt I had a startled look on my face. I asked her how she had acquired them from the angels.

6

The Presence of Angels at Death

For the Lord himself will come down from heaven, with a loud command, with the voice of the archangel and with the trumpet call of God, and the dead in Christ will rise first.

1 Thessalonians 4:16

When I was a small child traveling in the car with my parents, I would usually fall asleep in the backseat before we reached our destination. There was something about a moving car that always lulled me to sleep. Although my last memory of the day was happily looking out the window of the car, I would awaken in the morning safely tucked into my warm bed, carried there by my strong, loving father.

Writing this evokes the warm feelings of my dad's protective care. He never left me alone in the car in the dark on a cold winter's night. He would carry me to safety inside my home. I hope that dying will be similar to that experience, surrounded by the warmth and love of my family. I will go to sleep in peace and awaken in my forever home, carried there by God's angels. In Shakespeare's *Hamlet*, his friend Horatio says, "Good night sweet prince: / And flights of angels sing thee to thy rest!" In God's plan, we are carried by His angels to our eternal home, where we are presented to Jesus and the hosts of heaven with exuberant joy and celebration.

Many people I have counseled still carry unresolved grief several years after their loss. They are still clinging to their departed husband, wife, child or parent. In some convoluted way of thinking, they believe their loved one can be kept alive if they hold on to the pain. God is prevented from filling that sorrowful space in their hearts because it is already filled with grief and pain. God desires to journey with us in the grieving process as we hand over our loved ones to His eternal care.

One of the common misconceptions about angels is that they appeared only to holy saints in biblical times, or to the mystics, or to extraordinary people like Joan of Arc. In our next story, an angel appears to a farmer's wife in southwest Missouri to open her eyes to the spiritual realm. In Marilyn's story, told to her by her mother, God sends not one but many angels to encourage her and others in their faith.

A Sweet Encouragement

One May I drove from my home in Kansas City to visit my parents at their farm in southwest Missouri. Following my recent divorce, I retreated there frequently. While I was sitting with them, my mother looked at my dad and said, "Should we tell her?"

Her words sent a chill down my spine. Had one of my parents been diagnosed with a fatal disease? My mom said matter-of-factly, "I saw an angel." I was surprised. My family did not talk about spirits, angels or anything else that could be perceived as supernatural. The following account is from her diary:

Something very unusual happened to me this evening. I was dozing on the sofa when something woke me. I opened my eyes to see a bright light followed by a bright blue ball.

A little girl, who appeared to be about eight years old, stood on the rug beyond the edge of the sofa. I am sure she was an angel. She was very small, with shoulder-length blonde hair. Her nose was tiny, her face sweet. She was wearing a midlength white dress with a high neck and long sleeves. She had high lace-up black shoes. I did not see wings, nor did I see her hands. As we looked at each other, she cocked her head to one side and pursed her lips. She stood there for thirty seconds, and then she disappeared, seeming to fly through the door at the opposite end of the room. The blue glow followed her.

A couple of weeks later, I became very ill with double pneumonia and was taken to the hospital. I thought of the little angel often. She seemed to give me inner strength and encouragement. I know she helped me get well. I am positive now that there is a God and angels in heaven.

I was amazed that these supernatural visitations did not stir up any fear in a woman who kept the doors locked for fear of intruders. "I just hope she comes back some-day," my mother often said.

When my mother was 84 and very frail, she moved into a nursing home. One day, as I was sitting with her, she looked at me and said, "Oh, they are so beautiful."

"What is beautiful?" I inquired.

"The angels. They're all around me," she said. "And I want to go with them. Oh, I want to go. Please ask God to let me go." She had a look on her face as if she was seeing the most beautiful beings.

My mom passed away very peacefully ten days later, with my father, brother and me by her side. I think the reason Mom had these experiences is be-cause God knew she would accept them and share them, so that anyone who is wondering if there is such a place as heaven would be reassured.

—Marilyn Riley Mongan

Thirteen years after Marilyn's mom had her first encounter with an angel when she was at that liminal space—the thresh-old between this life and the next—God sent His faithful servant many glorious and bright angels to be her heavenly escort. Her obvious joy allowed her family to release her and bless her on her way.

I want to share a two-part story that carries a special mean-ing for Jeff, a former member of our staff. One September, Christian Healing Ministries held a weeklong conference in Michigan. On Tuesday evening, I was with Linda Strickland, my assistant at the time, and we were ministering to those who had come for prayer. As we prayed, we could feel God's holy presence. Several people came to us later and said, "Your singing is so beautiful!"

We were puzzled by their enthusiastic praise because we had not been singing. We both said, "It wasn't us." We had also heard the beautiful singing but were too engrossed in the prayer time to find the source. The music and the voices were incredible, although we could not understand the language.

When we discovered that the singing was not coming from the people at the conference, we realized we had been in the presence of angels who were worshiping God.

Apparently, everyone at the conference that evening heard the glorious music of heaven. After we returned home we learned the story within this story from Jeff.

Jeff's Vision of Angelic Choirs

I had surgery for colon cancer on August 24. After I returned home from the hospital, my parents planned to come to Jacksonville from south Florida on September 3 (Labor Day). But early that morning, my beloved mother suffered a severe stroke while she was sleeping.

My wife, Mary Ellen, and I drove to see her that same day. We stayed with my mom until Wednesday and then returned home. A few days later I had a vision: I saw that when the time came for my mom to die, all the members of the choirs she had been in or led would be there to welcome her to heaven with singing. I shared this with several friends.

Mom died the following week, the same week several Christian Healing Ministries staff members were in Michigan. When Linda returned from the

conference, she shared with us over dinner the delightful story of the angels singing that Tuesday
night.

I stopped eating and asked her, "What time was
that?"

"It was at nine o'clock."

That was the exact day and time that my mom
died. I fully believe that the angels singing at the
conference were the choir of heaven welcoming my
mom into the Kingdom. The vision I was given was
confirmed in this powerful way and has always been a
great comfort to me ever since her death.

—Jeff Sampson

Jesus said, "I go to prepare a place for you" (John 14:2
KJV). Throughout Scripture the theme is the same: We serve
a God who not only prepares a place for us, but also prepares
us for what is to come. Due to Jeff's difficult circumstances
related to his colon cancer and treatments, enduring his
mother's illness and death was very difficult. The comfort
of his vision allowed Jeff to know that God was in all of
these circumstances.

A common thread that runs through these stories is that
angels often prepare those who are involved in the loss of a
loved one. Angels come to give us strength and the courage
to let go of loved ones we so desperately want to hold forever
close to our hearts. This process ultimately involves more
than just letting go; it means entrusting or handing over a
loved one to God's care. Just as a parent releases or hands
over a beloved daughter to a young husband at her wedding,

so we have to find the strength to relinquish to Jesus our loved ones whom He is calling home.

Todd's family is given a glimpse of heaven when an angel appears as he is passing from this life. Before Todd takes his last breath, he and his loved ones are given strength, comfort and the assurance of God that all is in His great care.

Through the Eyes of a Child

When my son Todd was gravely ill with stage four melanoma, our family gathered to be with him in what seemed to be his last days. He was only thirty years old, and it was extremely difficult for me to watch him deteriorate. One night his little son, Christopher, who was about two and a half years old and had never said anything of the sort, said "Look, there is an angel over Daddy." The next morning Todd went on to be with the Lord.

—Barbara S. Reinmuth

Angels surround us as we release our loved ones for the journey to God. Heaven is a real place but a different dimension. Lord, give us eyes of faith to see and believe like a child.

Angels are assigned to assist the faithful during the transition from this life to the fuller life of their eternal home. As we let go of what binds us to our earthly existence, the things we consider so important will fade away. Concurrently, the angels are ready to escort us to our new home where we will dwell together with God and His heavenly hosts, and with the saints who have preceded us. Death is simply a transition to a fuller life for the believer. As the end of our time on earth approaches, angels surround us to prepare us for that last journey.

Just as the angels accompany us throughout this life, they will also care for us lovingly during our final transitions.

In *Angels: God's Secret Agents* (Doubleday, 1975), the Reverend Billy Graham writes that "death for the Christian cuts the cord that holds us captive in this present evil world so that angels may transport believers to their heavenly inheritance." Reverend Graham goes on to say that "death is robbed of much of its terror for the true believer, but we still need God's protection as we take that last journey." He explains that

> Christians should never consider death a tragedy. Rather he or she should see it as the angels do: They realize that joy should mark the journey from time to eternity. The way to life is through the valley of death, but the road is marked with victory all the way. Angels revel in the power of the Resurrection of Jesus, which assures us of our resurrection and guarantees us a safe passage to heaven.

As we shall see in chapter 8, the night before Jesus' death while He was praying in the Garden, an angel came to bring Him strength for what lay ahead. If *Jesus* needed the angel, how much more do *we* need their companionship! Not only do angels bring comfort and peace to the dying person, they often bring comfort to those who are grieving.

When the thief on the cross next to Jesus hung dying, he responded to what he saw in Jesus by saying, "'Jesus, remember me when you come into your kingdom.' Jesus answered him, 'I tell you the truth, today you will be with me in paradise'" (Luke 23:42–43).

These words of Jesus to the dying thief echo His words earlier to Martha at the tomb of her brother, Lazarus. Jesus had restored life to Lazarus after he had been dead for several days, and Jesus made a monumental statement: "I am the resurrection and the life. He who believes in me will live, even though he dies; and whoever lives and believes in me will never die" (John 11:25–26).

Jesus' promise that our spirits will never die helps us to understand that death is the *threshold* of the door to our heavenly home with Him. When we die, we enter into another dimension separated from our current reality by a thin veil. As we approach death, our spiritual eyes are opened, and we become conscious of the new life around us. Our spiritual senses begin to see into the fullness of God's Kingdom that surrounds us, and the things of this world slowly ebb away. Paul calls the body a tent (see 2 Corinthians 5:1) and an earthen jar of clay, the container that holds the spirit (see 2 Corinthians 4:7). When the issues of this earthly life are resolved, many experience the freedom to concentrate on the remarkable visual presence that envelops them.

I have heard so many stories about end-of-life experiences involving angels or angelic choirs singing celestial music and surrounded by brilliant lights. The dying person may see Jesus Himself or a departed loved one, and may express incredible feelings of joy and peace. Great comfort and life-giving hope are also brought to grieving loved ones. Struggling ceases as angels accompany those crossing over to the other side.

Angels were sent to many people in the Bible to announce an upcoming birth, but they also come to prepare us for death. These announcements can come concerning our own deaths or before the death of a beloved family member or friend. In the following account, an angel gently prepares two siblings for their mother's release.

Angel Announcing Death

In 2008, an angel visited my sister and me as we sat by our beloved mother's sickbed. The angel told us that our mother did not have much time left. We looked at our mother, then back to where the angel had been, but he was gone. This provided us with great comfort, as we knew that God was with us in the time of our mom's passing.

Years later I bought your book *Angels Are for Real* and read through it a few times. I started praying the prayers on pages 80, 120 and 195 every night before going to bed. One of my experiences with an angel happened on a February evening, when I awoke late at night to see a beautiful red glow coming from the living room. Soon I realized that there was a radiant angel with outstretched wings standing in the room. After the angel left I went back to a peaceful sleep. Following the angel's visit many wonderful things happened. The visitation seemed to mark the beginning of a better time in my life. It served as an encouraging nudge from the Lord to embrace the goodness of life.

—Michael Schutz

I have been with several people during the last hours of their earthly lives. The way they lived on this earth was reflected in the way they died. Those who trusted God in their lives tended to trust Him fully in death. "Precious in the sight of the LORD is the death of his saints" (Psalm 116:15).

An Angel Comforts a Dying Man

Joseph was eighty years old when he graduated into glory. He had worked for the City of San Francisco as a trolley car operator and as a sign painter for businesses around the city and loved to tell stories of his adventures in the big city. He was a wonderful storyteller. He was a man of great faith and shared with anyone who was willing to listen. Many souls were saved on his trolley car. Joseph raised his family in the presence of the Lord and served our Lord faithfully for twenty years as a deacon in our church, providing care to anyone in need.

When his health began to fail, the time came for Joseph to shift from being deacon and caregiver to patient and care-receiver. His cancer metastasized throughout his body and left him with little choice.

Hospice care began in the living room of his home. He received a prognosis of having only three months to live. We gathered around Joseph almost every day for prayer. These times were filled with God's mercy, love and comfort.

Joseph was fully conscious up to his last moments. He thanked each one of us for our love, care and support. Then he looked up into the vaulted ceiling above his bed and said, "Do you see that beautiful angel?" He smiled, relaxed into deep peace and soon after, he passed away.

I will never forget Joseph, nor his vision of the
angel. I believe God sends these holy companions to
help us transition into the next life with him.

—Rev. Keith Knauf

Joseph lived his entire life for others, sharing his deep
faith freely with everyone he encountered. During his final
moments he was graced to see the beautiful angel who was
waiting to carry him to God. Not only did he see the angel,
but he was filled with the peace and joy that was brought by
the angelic presence. For the dying person, these appearances
bring assurance that he or she is transcending this life. The
family and friends also receive comfort and strength, as we
see in this next story about Anna, who is a 101-year-young
grandmother when angels come for her.

A Grandmother's Passing

My grandmother Anna Pederson was 101 years
young when her century-old heart finally began to
slow down. She was in good health with a sharp
mind, but her heart could no longer keep up with her
body's demands. I was at her bedside with my older
sister, Janet, and some other family and friends when
her time approached.

I remember placing my grandmother's hand on
top of mine as she lay in her bed, semiconscious. She
was calling out the name of Jesus, tossing her head
back and forth and furrowing her brow. She was
passing from this life and seemed to be more aware
of the unseen realm. Her hand slowly became cold
and clammy as I prayed for her. Then I felt a physical

sensation that is difficult to explain. It was more than warmth and was intensely real. It felt like a warm energy, a presence. I believe an angel was in the room filling my spirit with light.

With my hand still under my grandmother's, it felt as though she was passing something on to me. She was a woman of deep prayer. She was Danish and was known to call herself a Viking, a fitting title for a woman of her mettle who had experienced much heartache within her family, yet always prayed and leaned on God to help her loved ones.

A second time, right after she passed away, I felt that same incredible light pass through me. It was powerful and tremendously loving, and filled my grieving heart with hope. I am forever grateful to the angel who came to be with us in Grandmother Anna's last moments.

—Cindy Incorvaia

What comes to me as I read this story of Anna and Cindy is the significance of the graces that were passed to this granddaughter from her grandmother. In her sorrow, she was comforted by the light and presence of an angel; in addition, she was also receiving her spiritual inheritance from her deeply faithful grandmother. According to Scripture, the rich legacy of faith-filled believers passes down from generation to generation. What a blessing!

In the following intimate story, a daughter and her beloved father are preparing for him to die. I believe most of us can relate to the daughter's attempts to guide her father on this frightening path. Having unresolved inner wounds has left darkness in his spirit that, along with a residue of pain, torments him as he approaches the end of life.

Comfort for a Dying Father

My husband, Tom, and I had been prayer group leaders for twenty years and had witnessed God's loving touch many times. We had always marveled at His timing.

It was in early December, and my father, Tony Strycharz, sat at the kitchen table in his home in Rhode Island trying to understand the illness that had overtaken him. He had battled for his life several times in his 78 years. He knew poverty, the hard labor of a steel worker and then a long bout with leukemia. He had always made the best of his life and showed a joyful face to the world, keeping his inner hurts largely masked.

Diagnosed with lung cancer and given only a short time to live, he was now battling for his life once again. This time, though, he was losing. He sat in front of me as I awkwardly tried to pray with him. Why was it so difficult to share God with my father when it was easy to do so with friends and even strangers? He simply did not understand that he was in the process of dying. As a look of pain came over his face I asked if there was anything I could do. His answer surprised me. He said, "Wanda, there's a figure always standing behind me, always wearing black, and he scares me."

I asked if he would like me to pray for the figure to go away, and he agreed. I closed my eyes, asked the

Holy Spirit how to pray and felt led to command the figure to leave in the name of God.

When I finished praying, I asked if the figure in black had gone. "Yes," he said, "but there is someone else standing behind me, dressed in white."

"Are you still afraid?" I asked him.

"No," he replied, "I'm at peace."

I asked my father if he would like to know the name of his guardian angel. Without hesitation, my father said yes. As we prayed, a name came to me—Harry. In less than a week, Dad's condition had worsened to the point that he needed the care of a nursing home. As we pushed his gurney onto the elevator of the nursing home, a man in a wheelchair joined us. This man kept looking over at my dad and finally asked, "That's not Tony, is it?"

The man had wonderful memories of my dad from years ago. He told us that he was a deacon in the Episcopal church and asked if he could spend time praying with Dad.

We were filled with God's love and care for each of us in this very difficult time in our lives. I asked the man in the wheelchair his name. It was—you guessed it—*Harry*. My father left this earth two days later. His guardian angel was clearly there to smooth Dad's way in the transition between life and death.

—Wanda Strycharz Eastham

People who come to Christian Healing Ministries for healing prayer frequently experience angels, often for the first time. Angels appear in various ways—sometimes as golden flecks of light or brilliant light that is not of this world, or as luminous beings standing beside them. Others transmit profound feelings of peace, joy or strength. Our experienced prayer ministers have countless angel stories and have had many life-changing experiences themselves. One of our Christian Healing Ministries prayer ministers told me the following story after visiting an eight-year-old cancer patient.

Devoted Angel

When I arrived at the home, I was met at the door by the little boy's mother, who was crying. She ushered me into the room where her beautiful son was sleeping in a chair. As we began to pray for him, an indescribable peace came over us. I looked down at the sleeping boy and suddenly became aware of a huge angel standing protectively behind him. The angel was so tall that his head touched the ceiling, yet he was pure spirit, almost clear, like a spirit with mass. I did not see wings or a halo, which is what I assumed would be aspects of this incredible being. The angel was focused on this precious sick boy. The angel's large hand covered the boy's chest as though he was imparting the light of heaven to the boy through his touch. As I stared at the angel's hand, I became aware of his strength, yet there was also an ever-present tenderness.

As I knelt to pray, I knew that this child was in the strong care of our loving God. The angel's presence ushered heaven into the room. A great peace washed over the little group that was gathered to join the angels in releasing this precious boy to God.

As someone entered the room I looked away for an instant, and when I looked back, I could no longer see the angel. I knew, however, that he was still with us. A short time later, that devoted angel guided his charge to his eternal home.

—Bob Bauwens

This child's angel came to take him to the place that God had prepared for him. In the gospel of John, Jesus comforted His disciples by telling them,

> "Do not let your hearts be troubled. Trust in God; trust also in me. In my Father's house are many rooms; if it were not so, I would have told you. I am going there to prepare a place for you. And if I go and prepare a place for you, I will come back and take you to be with me."
>
> John 14:1–3

The following story is a vivid reminder that God in His mercy cares for those of us who struggle with seemingly unanswered prayers.

Radiant Angel Brings Comfort

I was active in the church, even teaching Sunday school. One of our young parishioners, a twelve-year-old boy, was suffering from terminal leukemia. To my dismay, I heard that the church, led by the pastor, had been praying for the boy to die quickly. This seemed entirely wrong to me, so I urged the pastor to pray for healing instead. He looked at me with confusion, explaining that the boy had a terminal condition and was suffering. I received similar responses from other church members.

Still hopeful, I continued to pray and fast for the child's healing. On the fourth morning of my fast, the news that the boy had died was announced at church. At the Holy Communion service held in his memory, I could sense a prevailing sadness in the congregation, but I took comfort knowing that God's will ultimately prevails.

Back at home, I tried to return to my daily chores, but I found it impossible to stop thinking of the young boy. After putting our children to bed that night, I tried to find the energy to go into the kitchen to wash the pile of dirty dishes. All at once I felt apprehension about going into the kitchen, as though someone was in there waiting for me. I told myself I was being ridiculous, but the feeling persisted.

Finally, fighting my fear, I walked into the kitchen. What I saw shocked me. There, standing in my little kitchen, was a giant figure radiating pure, intense, golden light. The angel was so tremendously bright that I could not make out the facial features. I was so overcome with sheer surprise that I had to grip the edge of the sink.

The radiant angel communicated clearly—without speaking a word—that he had a message for me. Shining forth from the brilliant light was the child who had just died. The angel nudged him, as if the boy needed encouragement. With some reluctance, he said, "Thank you."

The angel gently drew the boy back into the light, into which he disappeared. All this time I was still gripping the sink, overwhelmed with the vision of this heavenly being. Then, ever so gently, I felt myself being lifted and carried into the living room. My Bible lay open on the end table next to the couch. The angel somehow "illuminated" a specific passage: "Even if one should rise from the dead, they would not believe" (see Luke 16:31).

A great peace washed over me. I knew that God had answered my prayer by giving me a glimpse of what heaven held for His children.

—H. T.

Angels Bring Glimpse of a Loved One

My grandmother Ruth Fiske never had any sons. But when her daughter—my mother—got married to my dad, this new son-in-law became like her own son. She adored him and he adored her, a gem in the world of in-law relations. To our shock, my dad suddenly and unexpectedly passed away from an aneurysm. When the doctor told us he had died, the first words out of my mom's mouth were, "Oh, no! How am I ever going to tell Nana? This will devastate her." When Ruth learned of my dad's passing, she took the news very poorly. As we had feared, she fell into a deep depression that held on for a long time.

A year later, on the anniversary of my dad's passing, I attended a Christian conference and went to a team for prayer on behalf of my grandmother to be healed of her depression. The person praying for me saw a vision of my dad with Jesus, which brought me great peace.

After the conference, I went to visit my mom and gave her a detailed account of what had happened. She told me excitedly that my grandmother had had a profound spiritual experience at exactly the same time that I was receiving prayer.

She told me that Grandmother was at home when the doorbell rang. Answering the door, she was stunned to see my smiling father standing between two large luminous angels. My father communicated with her without using any words—as if she could hear his thoughts. He told her that the slacks (which she had misplaced) were in a suitcase on the top shelf of her bedroom closet.

She hurried to the closet, where she found her missing slacks. Putting them on, she ran back to the living room. My dad and the angels were still standing there smiling. A few moments later they disappeared.

My grandmother was speechless over the whole incident. This angelic encounter brought her tremendous peace. The long-term depression lifted never to return. Her faith in God's loving care increased. She lived out the remainder of her life knowing that one day she would be joining her son-in-law with Jesus and the angels in heaven.

—Jean Bruce

The angels' visit brought healing to Ruth's deep depression. When God allowed that brief encounter, that glimpse into heaven, Ruth obtained the closure her heart needed to go forward. The fact that Ruth was directed to find her lost slacks is such a personal and caring touch. Perhaps her son-in-law was demonstrating that he still loved her and wanted to give her hope that they would be reunited in God someday.

Lorraine, another close friend of our family for many years, shares a story of how God places her in the path of a kind man who needs prayer when he is dying.

Angels Comfort Dying Man

I was driving to the school where I am a teacher. I was feeling very joyful, singing hymns of praise. As I got closer to school, I asked the Lord, "Why are Your angels at school today?" I could sense that there were thousands of them surrounding the school. I did not see them, but sensed them.

As I walked through the front door, I was still enjoying the feeling of being surrounded by angels. I said hello to a man, a stranger standing by the gym door. He smiled. I walked down the hall to drop some things off in a classroom. When I came back, I saw the same man writhing in pain on the floor. I knew instantly that the angels were there to bring comfort to this man.

I dropped to the floor and cradled him in my arms, praying all the while. The man died in my arms soon after. I feel sure that he died in peace, joyfully surrounded by the angels.

I did not know at the time if this man believed in Jesus, but I soon discovered from his wife that he spent much of his time at the local diner talking to his friends about—you know who—Jesus. He was a Christian. As always, God takes care of His children.

—Lorraine Greski

In the face of this man's death, we see the mercy of a loving God who did not allow His dear child to die alone. He was surrounded by loving angels and was cradled in the arms of a compassionate woman of deep faith who kept whispering encouraging prayers as he embarked upon his journey to heaven.

A Rainbow Bridge

Seven years ago, my mother (who lived in another state) was diagnosed with lung cancer. I would fly to visit her every three months. Even though we were praying for a miracle, over the course of a year and a half, her health continued to deteriorate. After watching her suffer so terribly, I changed my prayers. I had been asking God not to take her until I had the grace to let her go. But something began to change within me—I realized that my mother *needed* to be with God. No more pain. No more suffering. My prayer changed to: "Dear God, please let me be there when You take her home."

It was a Friday afternoon when the call came. My sister-in-law told me to take the next plane to Chicago, because Mom was not expected to make it through the night.

I managed to catch a flight fairly quickly. On the plane I was resting against the window. While look- ing at the sky, a radiant rainbow appeared. I knew at that moment that my mother had just died. I glanced at my watch and made note of the time.

The rainbow became a bridge to heaven upon which my mom was walking. Even though I could not see them, I sensed that there were angels lined up along both sides of the rainbow, all the way to heaven. They were singing and rejoicing, and the whole scene was a joyful celebration of her homecoming.

An incredible sense of peace came over me, and even though I knew that the next few days were going to be the most difficult days of my life, God in His mercy had taken the time to let me know that He did heal my mother—not in the physical sense, but spiritually.

When I got off the plane, I rushed to the hospital and found my mother's room. When I walked into the room I saw her body lying there. I felt my angel holding me up—surely I would have collapsed otherwise. I also felt a peaceful quietness in the dark room even though the rest of the hospital was quite busy. I knew that my mother was now finally resting in the arms of Jesus. Before I left the hospital floor, I asked what time my mother had died. Sure enough, it was when the rainbow had appeared in the sky.

—Winnie Christopher

Because angels are attentive to the entire family during the process of a loved one's death, they frequently concentrate their assistance where it is most needed. When Winnie first learned of her mother's illness, she experienced the enormous fear of profound loss. Having recently experienced a miracle of healing herself, she prayed expectantly for her mother to be healed of the cancer. During her struggle, Winnie experienced divine intervention that allowed her to realize that God was calling her mother to Himself, where all pain is transformed into new life. The sense she had on the airplane, of angels rejoicing as her mother crossed into heaven, filled her with incredible peace, and she knew that her mother was with Jesus.

The following account is from a good friend and minister who describes his preparation for his close friend's impending death.

Prepared for the End

My best friend was diagnosed with a form of cancer that has almost 100 percent morbidity. To combat the cancer, my friend had gone through radiation, chemo and brain surgery. He was a year into his battle with the illness. The surgery removed a major portion of his frontal lobe that controls language and emotions. His speech was limited to simple sentences.

He loved to worship, and when I was with him we would play worship CDs. We would sing in our prayer languages for extended periods of time while the worship music played, an activity that should have been physically impossible for him given his speech limitations. This was truly a spiritual gift. A few times, while we were worshiping, there was an overwhelming sense of others being present in the room. As we sang, the light level in the room became brighter, and a sweet aroma diffused the space. During these times, we could feel distinctly that we were part of another realm, one of heavenly worship with angels. Many times I would open my eyes, expecting to see someone in front of me because of the strong sense of a person standing near.

One night, during his illness, I had a dream in which my friend was lying asleep in a hospital bed, while I was sitting in a chair near him, praying. All of a sudden, a brilliant light shone into the room from above. I could hear the sound of angel wings and saw a large angel descend over his bed.

My friend, not with his own physical strength, stood on his bed and ascended toward the light as if drawn up into it. A voice said that he was going to be transferred but not physically transformed. I felt tremendous grief but also sensed the overwhelming compassion of the Father, because I realized he was going to be set free from his weakened body. I awoke, weeping.

Later I had another dream. I was in a great assembly of people who were worshiping God. There were angels everywhere—flying above the throne, playing instruments, standing guard. Still others were sounding drums and cymbals, and others were offering up containers of incense.

I could hear my friend beside me, singing at the top of his lungs. His appearance was different; he was no longer suffering from cancer. He was strong, full of life and smiling with great joy. Then he stopped, looked at me with his unique, quirky smile and exclaimed, "I'm outta here, bro!" I then became aware of some large, gentle and yet powerful hands resting on my shoulders, reassuring me as I watched him being escorted by angels. They were laughing with gusto. I awoke abruptly to a phone call. My friend had gone to be with the Lord that very morning.

—Robin Morrison

Once again we see the preparation of those involved in the transition of a loved one. We also find great comfort in the angelic visitations in the vivid dreams. A progression of hope came in the visions and dreams that were given by God to ease the sorrow of losing a dear friend. Dreams like these illuminate darkness and move us ever closer to the dwelling place of God where we are transformed from death to life.

Releasing a Beloved Father

My dad had been in our local hospital for nearly two weeks following quintuple heart bypass surgery that had gone reasonably well. He was 74. He had a lone kidney that was failing and a weakened heart.

Despite the health problems, he maintained his keen sense of humor and his kind temperament. Seeing his resilience, my mother and I were quite hopeful that he would soon be home.

My mother and I visited him in the hospital every day. One evening we kissed him and left to celebrate my mother's birthday.

Later that night, I got a phone call from a nurse, telling me that my dad was having trouble breathing. I asked if there was anything they could do to help him. The response was that they would do what they could. I prayed for a while and went to sleep. An hour later, the doctor called, asking if we wanted my dad to be resuscitated if he stopped breathing again.

It finally dawned on me that my dad was in serious trouble. I began praying intensely for him. I saw an image of Jesus standing next to my father at his hospital bed, gently leaning over him, speaking to him. I was comforted to see Him there, but sensed that He was preparing my dad to go with Him.

I knew that I needed somehow to *speak* to them. I know that people delay dying until they have permission from their families. I told Jesus He had my permission to take my dad. Then I spoke to my father in my heart, telling him tearfully that I loved him, but that it was all right for him to go with Jesus.

Shortly after, the phone call came: "Your father appears close to death. Can you come now?"

When we arrived at the hospital, the doctor said my dad had died fifteen minutes earlier. He asked if we would like some time alone with my dad's body. My friend Peg stayed in the hallway while my mother and I spent some quiet moments with him. He was so still. I put my hand over his heart and spoke to his spirit, telling him I loved him. I felt a brief flutter in his chest, but the doctor assured me he was gone.

When I stepped into the hallway, I heard a song throughout the small cardiac care unit. What an odd thing to hear at three a.m.! I recognized it as the same song our prayer group had recently learned. It was a simple chorus affirming, "Alleluia, Jesus is risen!"

Curious, I went around the medical unit, looking into each of the open bays. A few contained sleeping patients hooked up to the usual array of blinking monitors.

Finally, in a corner room, I found the source of this encouraging song. A healthy-looking middle-aged woman was sitting propped up in her bed with a cassette player next to her. Her bedside light was on. She was looking at me, smiling sweetly. Her smile and the song were heartwarming.

I have believed ever since that night that the smiling woman was an angel in human disguise, sent with a song to comfort my mother and me. What better song could one hear at the moment when your dear one has just died? A song that rejoices in the certainty of the Lord's triumph over death!

At Dad's funeral we shared memories of him, prayed for his rest and fittingly sang, "Alleluia, He is risen!"

—Pat Fitzgibbons

In the moments preceding her father's death, Pat was alerted by angels to pray for him and to release him to Jesus, who at that moment was speaking to him in his hospital room. As Pat spoke to her father's spirit, he seemed to receive the peaceful release he was waiting for. What was the brief flutter Pat felt in her dad's heart? In that hallowed moment, was that his heart saying "Good-bye—I love you, too"? I find that to be breathtakingly sacred—the forever love that passed between them as he found his way home with Jesus. Then in the midst of all her tangled emotions, Pat heard a song—played by a smiling angel—and the song was about resurrection. A beautiful angel brought hope, encouragement and a gentle reminder that because of Jesus she and her dad will enjoy eternity together.

7

Jesus: The Significance of Angels

Praise the LORD, you his angels, you mighty ones
who do his bidding.

Psalm 103:20

Whether Jesus was teaching, healing or casting out demons,
He moved purposely and easily between the two realms of
heaven and earth. His words and actions demonstrated a
remarkable authority over sickness, demons, death and the
natural world.

Jesus revealed clearly the importance of angels in the Kingdom of God throughout His ministry. In this chapter, I want
to share some Scriptures where Jesus Himself impressed on
us how integral angels are in the spiritual realm and the work
of God on earth.

151

Jesus encouraged His listeners to open their eyes to the invisible spiritual realm around them. He knew that they needed to shift their focus away from the worries and trials of this world to see the eternal things of God. He wanted His followers to know that they were not alone in life's battles. Jesus made it clear that the holy angels have an enormous effect on individuals and world events.

Sadly, we have largely failed to realize the vital presence of the angels. Nor do we completely recognize how God has given angels the authority *and* power to effect real change in our world. We can rely on the indwelling Holy Spirit to transform and renew us, and we have God's holy angels to accompany, guide and protect us. Angels are extremely active and involved in the Church and in the world!

My First Time Seeing Angels

I was attending a conference with people from all over the world. As we were worshiping God I heard a heavenly sound.

Suddenly angels were in our midst; I saw them! They were walking to the front of the church to stand alongside the musicians. I was so deeply touched to see them that I wept for joy.

Their forms were soft, white shapes, surrounded by an equally soft glow. Their wings were iridescent white with hints of lavender and pink. I could not see their faces.

I feel so blessed by God to have the privilege of seeing angels and to share this joy with others.

—Jean M. Jones

Angels in the Delivery Room

When I was in the delivery room giving birth, I was filled with anxiety. The doctor had given me a spinal block to ease my pain, but it did not ease my fears. Then, as I was praying, a deep peace filled me and a holy presence surrounded me.

I saw several dozen angels who seemed to be filled with joyful anticipation. They looked transparent, with hair and features that were feminine. They wore long, colorless, supple robes with arm-length sleeves. Elevated above the floor, they seemed to emit a living, moving stream of iridescent and dreamlike light.

I knew that they were assigned to protect me and my unborn child as the delivery progressed. The angels were looking toward one particular angel, who I believed was my baby's guardian angel. They had gathered to rejoice over this new life. As my daughter took her first breath, the angels disappeared from my sight, but their presence remained.

—Nina Sheffer

Large crowds gathered to hear Jesus teach. Among the crowds were tax collectors, sinners, Pharisees and teachers of the Law. Jesus told them three parables: the Parables of the Lost Sheep, the Lost Coin and the Lost Son. These stories revealed the *inclusiveness* of God's love for anyone who has been lost and who is found. This teaching was in direct contrast to the *exclusiveness* of the Pharisees and teachers of the Law. The message of God's great mercy, enduring love and forgiveness was affirmed in each parable.

Then Jesus made a radical statement: "I tell you that in the same way there will be more rejoicing in heaven over one sinner who repents than over ninety-nine righteous persons who do not need to repent" (Luke 15:7). Was Jesus giving us a glimpse of a joyful celebration with God, the saints, angels and the hosts of heaven? But might not that make God appear frivolous or too carefree? Sin is ruinous. Should we not take it more seriously?

To the sinners in the crowd, these stories illustrated and underscored a truth about God that had seldom been presented before: mercy and celebration with a loving Father. Jesus was allowing the people to catch a glimpse into the dazzling, joyful atmosphere of the angelic hosts of heaven.

Touched by Angels

I was attending a conference with Jamie Buckingham as the speaker. He was explaining what had happened to a woman who had been crying loudly during the previous service. She had experienced a visitation from angels. I, too, had been visited in somewhat the same way during one of the praise sessions. Like her, I began weeping almost uncontrollably. While praising God, with my hands uplifted, I saw flashing bright lights moving around the room. I knew angels were present.

—Pansy Smith

Angels Are Immortal

Jesus was asked a question by the Sadducees, who did not believe in resurrection. They asked about a certain woman who married seven brothers. Each died, and then she died. The Sadducees asked Jesus, "Whose wife will she be at the resurrection?"

> Jesus replied, "The people of this age marry and are given in marriage. But those who are considered worthy of taking part in that age and in the resurrection from the dead will neither marry nor be given in marriage, and they can no longer die; for they are like the angels."
>
> Luke 20:34–36

Immortality is the believer's destination—an eternity of love shared with God and His holy angels.

An Angel Beside Me

One morning, as I was sitting in my breakfast room reading Scripture, I started worshiping God. Suddenly I became aware of a presence in the room. When I opened my eyes I saw a tall, beautiful female angel. Her hands were folded in prayer, and she wore a cream-colored robe made of a stunning material that moved as if it were animated by some unseen force. Her hair was light brown and braided in a way that, as a hairdresser, I have never seen before. I started weeping and thanking God for the privilege of seeing her. I closed my eyes, and when I opened them she was gone.

Later that week, I began to feel the same strong presence. Standing beside me was the same angel with her hands folded in prayer. I have not seen her since then, but I know that she is always near. From

the first time she appeared I have had a feeling of
safety.

—Dolores Purvis

Angels Are Empowered to Bring Healing

Healing was central to the message of Jesus during the days
when He walked this earth and still is today. Jesus never
treated healing as a side issue. His mercy and compassion
compelled Him to restore health and life to everyone He
encountered. Angels also are often sent to bring healing to
those suffering emotionally, spiritually or physically. These
angels sent by God have been given the power necessary to
heal. As they draw near, the entire environment alters. The
gospel of John relates such a story.

Jesus had returned to Jerusalem and was visiting the pool
of Bethesda near the Sheep Gate. Family members would
bring their disabled and disease-stricken loved ones to the
pool, where they would spend the day waiting expectantly
for an angel to come and stir the water. They believed that
the first one into the pool after this stirring would be healed
of his or her disease (see John 5:4). This Scripture gives us an
important insight into the healing power of angels, whether
seen or unseen.

Unfortunately, the lame or paralyzed could not reach the
pool without assistance; one crippled man lay there waiting
for 38 years, perhaps from childhood. When Jesus saw him
lying there, He asked him, "Do you want to get well?" The
man explained that he had no one to help him get into the
pool first. Jesus said, "Get up! Pick up your mat and walk."
The man was cured instantly.

Angels by My Son

My son was critically ill and in the hospital. The doctors gave him little hope of recovery. While I was sitting by his bed praying, two angels appeared on either side of the bed. I felt that they had come to watch over him. They were dressed in flowing white garments and kept a countenance of complete calm.

These angels stayed by his side, and later, when his health seemed to be deteriorating, a third one appeared at the foot of his bed. Their presence gave me a feeling of deep peace, and I felt sure that he would recover. Within a short time my son had fully recovered. The doctors told my son that he would not be able to return to work but, praise God, he was back in his office in two weeks.

—Nancy Seeber

A Healing Angel

My seven-year-old daughter was sick with the flu and had a very high fever. Despite medication and prayer, her temperature remained high. My husband was working a late shift, so I was home alone with her. As I prayed I was overcome with assurance that she would be okay.

Within minutes, however, she began screaming, "Take me home!" I could tell she was delirious. Desperate for help, I prayed, "Jesus, I can't help her but You can."

I had an inner sense to praise the Lord, so I began to sing "Praise Him in the Morning." I do not know how long I sang, but after a time my daughter became peaceful. A few minutes later she said, "Mommy, she has a ring around her head."

"Who does, honey?" I asked.

"The angel." I turned to look in the direction of her gaze, but I saw nothing.

Later she told me that an angel had appeared to her while I was singing. She described the angel as being the same size as me, with long curly hair. She had wings and was wearing a white robe with a golden cross emblazoned on the front. The angel was suspended above the floor. My daughter also said that the roof disappeared and she could see the night sky. She said the angel disappeared when I looked at her. Her story always remains consistent.

—Claire Barton

Heavenly Glow

An angel brought peace to me during the most difficult time of my life. I was struggling through prolonged relationship problems while also feeling the weight of deep existential doubt concerning my basic purpose in life. Prayer offered some solace from the torments of my inner life, but I was desperate for a palpable sense of relief and hope.

Part of my weekend routine was to go to church each Saturday night to pray for the Sunday services. Tonight, however, my feelings of despair were growing more intense by the hour. I was at a loss as to how I could turn the tides in my increasingly grim situation.

When I arrived at church, I made my way into the dark, empty sanctuary. I began to tell God about the way I felt. Only a few seconds passed before I became aware of an unusual light in the sanctuary.

Curious, I turned to look at the source of this brightness. There in the front pew, in utter contrast to the surrounding darkness, was the figure of a man. He seemed to be lit from within, with a soft, white glow that flowed out in all directions. It was a beautiful sight. I did not feel even a hint of fear in his presence.

Next, this being of light gently pierced the deep silence that had collected in the sanctuary, speaking the words, "Everything will be okay. Do not worry so much."

I stood in silence, a bit mesmerized in the face of this unusual experience. The encouraging words came again, and I was filled with a sense of total calm. I knew that I was safe, and that I was not alone even in the worst of my struggles.

After a few seconds, he stood up and ascended the stairs to the balcony. He repeated the message a final time: "Everything will be okay." Having said this, he faded out of visibility, and I was once again alone in the sanctuary. This aloneness was different from before, because the unimpeachable presence of love and comfort that the angel carried still lingered in my spirit. I felt certain that this message of assurance had come mercifully from God, who knew the weariness of my soul and my heart's desire for freedom.

—Bill Reilly

Angels Escort Us at Death

Jesus told the crowd surrounding Him a story about a rich man who lived in luxury and a poor, sick man named Lazarus who sat begging at the gate every day (see Luke 16:19–31). The beggar was covered with sores and was so hungry that he waited to see if he could grab the rich man's table scraps before the dogs ate them. Jesus said that when Lazarus died the holy angels carried him gently to Abraham's side, a place of blessedness and the home of the righteous. When the rich man died there is no mention of an angel escort. Jesus said he was buried and was sent to a place of torment, with a great chasm separating him from Lazarus and from Abraham.

Many angel stories describe similarly how angels appear just before death to carry the departing one to heaven. "Precious in the sight of the LORD is the death of his saints" (Psalm 116:15).

Satan Will Test Our Faith

Just as Jesus interspersed His teaching with stories about God's holy angels, He also continued to warn His disciples about Satan and the fallen, unholy angels. In the gospel of John, in the last discourse, Jesus prayed for Himself, His disciples and for all believers—that includes you and me—to be protected from the evil one: "Holy Father, protect them by the power of your name—the name you gave me—so that they may be one as we are one. . . . My prayer is not that you take them out of the world but that you protect them from the *evil one*" (John 17:11, 15 emphasis added).

The Sound of a Whoosh

Early one summer my neighbor committed suicide. In the weeks that followed, I did my best to help his widow, who was suffering terribly. During that time, I began to experience feelings of extreme anxiety, which eventually affected my health. When I could not find any relief, it became clear to me that I was up against something that was much more powerful than I could handle.

One Sunday morning my pastor and several prayer ministers gathered around me to pray. I told them about the anxiety that had taken over my life. They discerned that I was being affected by a demonic presence due to what I had recently been through. I remember lying by the altar, crying out to God for help as they prayed for my freedom.

Shortly after the prayer began I heard what sounded like a great *whoosh* behind me, which made me think of a huge bird with outstretched wings. I felt free for the first time in weeks. I had been through an intense spiritual battle, but God had provided for me. After reading your book on angels, I realize that the sound I heard behind me came from the wings of a mighty angel sent to minister to me.

—Barbara Ebersole

Jesus was acutely aware of the unrelenting onslaught of the enemy in His own life and in the lives of His disciples. So He prayed for them to remain strong and to persevere in the battle with the protective covering of His name that is above every name—Jesus Christ!

161

A remarkable display of the loving concern of Jesus for His followers is seen at the Last Supper. A dispute arose among the disciples about which one of them was the greatest. Judas, whom Satan had already entered, was soon to betray Jesus for thirty pieces of silver. Jesus foresaw that Satan wanted to deceive His followers. When the conflict started, Jesus seized the moment to address the heart of the issue: contending for supremacy. Jesus said, "Simon, Simon, Satan has asked to sift you as wheat. But I have prayed for you, Simon, that your faith may not fail. And when you have turned back, strengthen your brothers" (Luke 22:31–32).

In Scripture, when a name is spoken, especially twice, it is usually an expression of tender love, coupled with a warning. Jesus was addressing Simon, but He was also warning all of the disciples to stay on guard against the enemy. Satan was asking permission, as he did with God about Job (see Job 1:6–12; 2:1–6), to be allowed to test Peter's faith, to see if he could cause him to fail. Jesus foresaw that Peter would deny Him three times. But the words Jesus spoke brought strength to Peter after the resurrection.

Mighty Angel

My pastor was going through a difficult time and seemed to be under spiritual attack. One Sunday night some members of our church gathered for prayer. I asked God to send angels to protect him. As we were praying, I looked up and saw a mighty angel walking up the main aisle to the pastor. His flowing robe was a golden cream color. His large wings glistened like gold and his hair was light brown. I thought that he could be an archangel.

He walked up the stairs and stood behind the pastor and enfolded him with his wings. The Lord was revealing to us that our pastor was under His protection, and that I need not worry, only pray. This was a great comfort to me.

—Dolores Purvis

This beautiful example of mercy and love should be a great encouragement to those of us who are under attack, or have failed, denied Jesus and fallen away. God is never surprised! We belong to Him, and no one can snatch us from His hands.

A Dark Presence

In your book *Angels Are for Real*, the chapter about fallen angels really helped me. I saw some disturbing things last summer that I now believe were evil spirits, but at the time, I did not know what to think. In bed one night, I saw menacing, black, misty shadows crawling toward me and making horrible hissing noises. I started kicking at them, but my foot went through them. Eventually they disappeared, but my encounter with evil was not over yet. Moments later, I saw a dark, looming shadow in the corner of my room. Suddenly it started floating toward me! Terrified, I closed my eyes and pulled the covers over my head. When I dared to look again, the figure was gone, but an eerie presence remained in my room. Later that night, while I was lying in bed, my hand was dangling near an air-conditioning vent, which was not on. I felt a rush of cold air across the top of my hand, and a voice said my name in a low, creepy whisper. As you can imagine, I was horrified. When I told my mom about it the next day, she advised me to wear a cross to bed. I have worn a cross every evening and have not encountered anything evil since that terrifying night.

—T. Reilly

Satan Will Be Banished Forever

Jesus encouraged His followers to take care of those who are hungry, thirsty, sick, strangers in need of shelter and clothing, and those in prison. He gave them an illustration, concluding, "Whatever you did for one of the least of these brothers and sisters of mine, you did for me" (Matthew 25:40). He made it clear, however, that if we do not do these things for the needy, we will experience the same punishment as Satan and his demons: "Depart from me, you who are cursed, into the eternal fire prepared for the devil and his angels" (Matthew 25:41).

In the book of Revelation, the final battle ensues. This is the epic battle between good and evil. The angels are the mighty warriors glorifying and praising God and bringing evil to a final conclusion. Scripture describes how at one point the great archangel Michael and his angels are fighting against the dragon (Satan) and his angels. The holy angels, being superior in strength to the demonic realm, cast Satan out of the heavenlies (see Revelation 12:7–9).

The final end of Satan is described: "And the devil, who deceived them, was thrown into the lake of burning sulfur, where the beast and the false prophet had been thrown. They will be tormented day and night for ever and ever" (Revelation 20:10).

Angel with Flashing Lightning and Fire

One morning I received a call from a friend. Her mother lived with her and had suddenly fallen ill and needed to go to the doctor. She asked if her daughter could come play with my daughter, Jennifer, and the other children playing in my yard.

My friend Laurie arrived and told me worriedly to bring the children inside. She had seen a man standing on the wooded side of my property. When he saw her he quickly got into his car, which was still parked on my street. I brought all the children inside and made sure all the doors were locked. I looked out the window and saw him drive off.

That evening Jesus gave me a vision. I saw an angel that looked like flashing lightning and fire swiftly coming down. Sword in hand, the angel struck the dark figure that had been on my property.

The next morning, when I was reading the Bible, it fell open to Psalm 34:7: "The angel of the Lord encamps around those who fear him, and he delivers them." I thank God for His faithfulness, protection and love.

—Cindy McCabe

This promise is for the righteous:

Now the dwelling of God is with men, and he will live with them. They will be his people, and God himself will be with them and be their God. He will wipe every tear from their eyes. There will be no more death or mourning or crying or pain.

Revelation 21:3–4

Angels Will Take a Prominent Role in Judgment

In Matthew 13, Jesus used parables to teach His followers: the Parables of the Sower, the Weeds, the Mustard Seed, the Yeast and the Net. Jesus said that these parables contain the secrets of the Kingdom of God. He used vivid imagery to explain that the angels of God will be very active at the end of the age.

Battle in the Night

During a time of great change in my life, I was experiencing tremendous anxiety that made it difficult for me to sleep. One night I was overwhelmed with panic. I wanted to pray, but I could not breathe deeply enough to do so. I remember whispering "Jesus," and immediately became aware of a spiritual battle taking place in my room. I could not see anything, but I could feel the struggle between light and dark forces. I was stunned by the revelation that I was being protected by Jesus and His angels. At a time when I felt most weak and vulnerable, He was there in strength and power.

After some time the room became still. I was no longer anxious and was able to fall asleep. While that experience did not entirely eradicate anxiety from my life, it most definitely changed me. I knew God and the angels were battling against the enemy on my behalf.

—Lesley Cooley Walsh

In the Parable of the Weeds, angels separate the wheat from the weeds in a field, removing everything that was sowed there by the farmer's enemy (see Matthew 13:24–43). Jesus explained the meaning: At the end of the age, the angels will come into the world and separate the wicked from the righteous. Good and evil will no longer be allowed to coexist. The seeds were sowed either by God or by the devil. Now the angel harvesters will come and separate them according to their deeds, which are known to the angels: "I tell you," Jesus said, "whoever acknowledges me before men, the Son of Man will also acknowledge him before the angels of God" (Luke 12:8).

Later in the book of Matthew, Jesus began to prepare His followers for the signs of His return and the end of the age. They probably realized the time was approaching quickly because they responded to Him with questions about the end. The negative forces were gathering strength against Jesus and His ministry, and undoubtedly against His disciples. Jesus warned them about false christs, false prophets, wars and rumors of wars, nation rising against nation, famines, earthquakes and increased wickedness.

Then He turned to His disciples and revealed their destiny on earth: They would be persecuted, hated and killed— all because they followed Him. These were not words of comfort. Jesus was being brutally honest. He knew that they needed to know about the coming times in order to be prepared and not deceived. He was warning them ahead of time.

He said, after the distress of those days,

> "The sign of the Son of Man will appear in the sky, and all the nations of the earth will mourn. They will see the Son of Man coming on the clouds of the sky, with power and great glory. And he will send his angels with a loud trumpet call,

and they will gather his elect from the four winds, from one end of the heavens to the other."

Matthew 24:30–31

This image has been captured graphically by artists throughout the ages: the angel sounding the trumpet; the dead in Christ rising out of their graves; the living either caught up into glory by the holy angels or descending into darkness—pulled down by demons to spend eternity. This is the Last Judgment: Jesus, accompanied by the great archangel Michael and all the hosts of heaven, arriving to reclaim His Kingdom. Jesus reminded His disciples that "no one knows about that day or hour, not even the angels in heaven, nor the Son, but only the Father" (Matthew 24:36; see 1 Corinthians 15:51–58).

Angels Overpower Demons

Several years ago I had a simple procedure to remove a mole that was growing on my scalp. I had known the doctor for years, and his nurse and I attended the same church. The doctor injected a local anesthetic at my hairline. That is the last thing I remember. Much later I awoke with the nurse repeatedly calling my name. The concerned doctor told my husband, "It shouldn't have done that to her. It was only a local." I was extremely weak and felt some soreness around my ankles, but with help I managed to walk.

After returning home, I shared with my husband what I had experienced. I remember being in a dark, frightening place, trapped in a spiral with several evil beings. These murmuring, grotesque things were holding my ankles and pulling me down. With all my strength I struggled to free myself but I could not. I was being sucked into utter darkness.

Suddenly, strong, gentle angels pulled me upward, away from my tormenters. Though the angels were pulling strongly on my wrists, it did not hurt, as their touch was tender. I could not see them, but I could feel their urgent desire for my well-being. Finally, the demons released me and the angels pulled me out of the spiral. I have always believed in angels and have had other angelic encounters, but this was the most dramatic and life-changing.

—Dianne H.

Angels are not fantastical, mythical creatures. From beginning to end, angels inhabit a high place of prominence in God's plan for all of us. They are ever-present with us and come to our aid when God commands them. Jesus, in looking ahead, told us about their part in the glorious consummation that He promised would come at the end of time. How comforted we should be to know that God in His infinite wisdom will send these superb beings to help us! "For the Son of Man is going to come in his Father's glory with his angels, and then he will reward each person according to what he has done" (Matthew 16:27).

8

Angels in the Life of Jesus

And again, when God brings his firstborn into
the world, he says, "Let all God's angels worship him." In speaking of the angels he says, "He
makes his angels winds, his servants flames of
fire."

Hebrews 1:6–7

Jesus Christ is the centrality and embodiment of Christianity.
All biblical accounts, beliefs, doctrines, traditions and prac-
tices of the Christian faith revolve around the foretelling and
the birth, life, death and resurrection of Jesus.

In the past God spoke to our forefathers through the prophets
at many times and in various ways, but in these last days he
has spoken to us by his Son, whom he appointed heir of all
things, and through whom he made the universe. The Son is
the radiance of God's glory and the exact representation of
his being, sustaining all things by his powerful word. After

he had provided purification for sins, he sat down at the right hand of the Majesty in heaven.

Hebrews 1:1–3

We tend to think of Jesus, when He lived on earth in human form, as invulnerable and undefeatable. And He was. He was and is the Son of God incarnate. Scripture says, "Jesus Christ is the same yesterday and today and forever" (Hebrews 13:8).

Yet Jesus was also a human being in all ways, except that He was without sin. He experienced the same humanity that we do. And in His times of danger, suffering, weakness and fatigue here on earth, God sent holy angels to His aid. Even before Jesus' conception, the mighty archangel Gabriel was given the charge concerning His future conception and birth.

The Visitation

The archangel Gabriel was entrusted with the greatest message of all time, given to a young virgin named Mary in the small village of Nazareth in Galilee. This message would radically change the course of human history.

> God sent the angel Gabriel to Nazareth, a town in Galilee, to a virgin pledged to be married to a man named Joseph, a descendant of David. The virgin's name was Mary. The angel went to her and said, "Greetings, you who are highly favored! The Lord is with you." Mary was greatly troubled at his words and wondered what kind of greeting this might be. But the angel said to her, "Do not be afraid, Mary, you have found favor with God. You will be with child and give birth to a son, and you are to give him the name Jesus. He will be great and will be called the Son of the Most High.

172

The Lord God will give him the throne of his father David, and he will reign over the house of Jacob forever; his kingdom will never end."

"How will this be?" Mary asked the angel, "since I am a virgin?" The angel answered, "The Holy Spirit will come upon you, and the power of the Most High will overshadow you. So the holy one to be born will be called the Son of God."

Luke 1:26–35

Mary's yes echoes throughout time: "I am the Lord's servant," Mary answered. "May it be to me as you have said" (Luke 1:38).

When Jesus was conceived, He became God incarnate. The second Person of the Trinity became flesh in Mary's womb, miraculously conceived by the power of the Holy Spirit. Through the incarnation, the divine nature of the Son (while remaining God) was seen as being united with human nature in one divine person. From the time of His conception, Jesus was both fully man and fully God. His birth by a virgin fulfilled the Old Testament prophecies about the salvation of the world—Immanuel: God with us!

A second angelic appearance occurred after Mary revealed her pregnancy to Joseph, her betrothed husband. In those days, a betrothal was as legally binding as a marriage is today. Scripture reveals that Joseph, a carpenter, "was a righteous man and did not want to expose her to public disgrace, so he had it in his mind to divorce her quietly" (Matthew 1:19). They were legally bound to each other, but not yet husband and wife. Joseph knew the baby was not his child. He also knew that the punishment for infidelity prescribed by the Law was death by stoning.

This tore at Joseph's heart because he loved Mary, yet he could not accept her pregnancy. That changed when an angel, most likely Gabriel, visited Joseph in his first of several angelic dreams.

> But after he had considered this, an angel of the Lord appeared to him in a dream and said, "Joseph son of David, do not be afraid to take Mary home as your wife, because what is conceived in her is from the Holy Spirit. She will give birth to a son, and you are to give him the name Jesus, because he will save his people from their sins."
>
> Matthew 1:20–21

Joseph listened to the angelic guidance in his dream. "When Joseph woke up, he did what the angel of the Lord had commanded him and took Mary home as his wife. But he had no union with her until she gave birth to a son. And he gave him the name Jesus" (Matthew 1:24–25).

The Road to Bethlehem

When I reread the familiar account of Jesus' birth, I am struck by the way the sovereign hand of God orchestrated each event to provide safety for His Son. God's plan would not be altered by the Law, by the Roman emperor Caesar Augustus nor by Satan, the evil one. In order to situate Jesus' birth in Bethlehem and fulfill prophecy, the Holy Spirit prompted Caesar Augustus to order the first-ever census of the entire Roman Empire. God used a pagan emperor to fulfill the prophecy of Micah 5:2: "But you, Bethlehem Ephrathah, though you are small among the clans of Judah, out of you will come for me one who will be ruler over Israel, whose origins are from of old, from ancient times." Everyone was forced to travel to his or her place of birth in order to register. This meant that Joseph, who was a descendant of King David, had to travel to Bethlehem with Mary to register for the census.

The ninety-mile journey from Nazareth would have taken about ten days traveling on foot, and probably four days' travel by donkey or caravan. Mary, being in the final month of her pregnancy, would have found any type of travel extremely grueling. On my first trip to Israel I rode a donkey for a day and was fairly miserable because of the donkey's peculiar, jaunty gait. The following day every muscle in my body hurt. Mary had to walk or ride for many days! Without a doubt, she was a remarkable woman of faith, grace, strength and courage. At that moment in history the entire angelic realm must have been on high alert. Every movement, every threat was monitored by the angels' watchful protection. Warring angels under assignment from the archangel Michael battled the demonic forces attempting to threaten the life of the unborn Jesus.

The last part of the journey would have been the most difficult—traveling from Jericho (below sea level) to Bethlehem, which is 2,500 feet above sea level. Joseph must have been desperate to find a room for Mary, who was already in labor. Thousands of people were traveling to their hometowns to register. Available rooms were impossible to find in a small town of six hundred inhabitants. Over and over Joseph was turned away.

Tradition points to a limestone cave that served as a stable for animals as the birthplace of Jesus. The Church of the Nativity houses the cave where many believe Jesus was placed in the manger after His birth. Other researchers point to a family home where Joseph and Mary were given the lower floor where animals were kept. The Bible simply tells us that the newborn baby Jesus was placed in a manger.

The Shepherds and the Angels

Wherever Jesus was born, it was an angel of God who proclaimed the glorious good news. God chose lowly shepherds, tending their sheep in the fields near Bethlehem, to hear the most magnificent, triumphant announcement of all times: The Savior of the world had been born! These uneducated, simple shepherds received the message that would forever change human destiny. The shepherds were terrified as the glory of God filled the skies. But the angel reassured them and said,

> "I bring you good news of great joy that will be for all the people. Today in the town of David a Savior has been born to you; he is Christ the Lord. This will be a sign to you: You will find a baby wrapped in cloths and lying in a manger."
>
> Luke 2:10–12

Before the shepherds could even react, the entire blackened sky split open with the brilliant, blinding light of heaven. Then the voice of the angel was multiplied a thousand times over. Celestial music filled the quiet night—indescribable harmonies sung by voices with incredible range. As their eyes focused, the shepherds realized the dazzling light was the brilliance of the shining angels who filled the entire sky, thousands upon thousands praising God, unable to contain their overwhelming joy!

Luke describes it: "Suddenly a great company of the heavenly host appeared with the angel, praising God and saying, 'Glory to God in the highest, and on earth peace to [those] on whom his favor rests'" (Luke 2:13–14).

When the angels had gone back into heaven, the shepherds hurried to Bethlehem, where they found the Holy Family just as the angel had said. The shepherds told Mary and Joseph about the encounter with the angels and fell to their knees in wonder as they beheld Jesus in the manger. These poor, lowly shepherds became the first evangelists as they spread the good news: The Messiah has come!

The Good Shepherd

Even in His birth, Jesus was identified with the shepherds in the field who were protecting the sheep used for sacrifice in the Temple. Later, during His ministry, Jesus often referred to Himself as the good Shepherd. Jesus, the good Shepherd, "tends his flock. . . . He gathers the lambs in his arms and carries them close to his heart; he gently leads those that have young" (Isaiah 40:11).

"I am the good shepherd," Jesus said. "I know my sheep and my sheep know me—just as the Father knows me and I know the Father—and I lay down my life for the sheep" (John 10:14–15). The prophet Ezekiel referred to the Davidic Messiah who would shepherd His flock in the same way that God shepherds His people (see Ezekiel 34:12, 16).

Early one beautiful spring day, my friend Lynne and I decided to go camping in the Sinai desert in southern Israel. We arrived at our destination (which meant we stopped when we grew tired and hungry). There, with no one for miles around, we pitched our small tent at dusk, prepared a simple meal and settled in for the night. Lying on our backs, we were overwhelmed by the enormity, clarity and beauty of the desert sky. Without the lights and pollution of the city, we could see the brilliant stars, the depths of color and the magic of the night sky.

We were suddenly reminded of those long-ago drowsy shepherds lulled by the tinkling of the bells on the sheep in their charge. They were huddled around a campfire that kept them warm and protected them from predators. That night would have started out like so many other nights, when without warning a flaming angel appeared with the glorious good news.

I went to sleep in our tent that night reflecting on angels, shepherds and the Prince of Peace. I was awakened the following morning by the intense desert heat and by shuffling sounds coming from outside our tent. Unzipping the tent flap, I crawled outside right into the midst of a herd of sheep!

Approaching us from the edge of the herd was a young Bedouin shepherd girl who seemed delighted to see outsiders who had stumbled into her territory. Bedouins are desert dwellers who live in large mobile tents in the desert. They are an Arab ethno-cultural group, descendants from nomads who have historically inhabited the desert. About a hundred thousand live in Israel, and most are animal herders.

We could not believe we went to sleep talking about shepherds and woke up face-to-face with one *and* her entire herd.

This young girl, who looked about fourteen years old, had obviously spent the night alone in the desert with her flock. She was exotic looking, with layered clothing that was beautifully hand-stitched. Her head was covered but dark wisps of hair had slipped out. Her skin was deeply tanned by the desert sun, and she had a big, bright smile and eyes that danced with joy.

We could not speak each other's language, but that did not dampen her enthusiasm. We spent over an hour with her, gesturing and laughing. As interested as she was in us, I noticed she was totally aware at all times of the whereabouts of her sheep. Occasionally she would leave us to gather a wandering one back to the herd. Sometimes she made an unusual sound, talking to the sheep; other times, just a simple movement of her staff. Or she would pick up a young one, sensing it needed to be close to her. Her affection for her sheep was very evident.

Finally, she gestured for us to come with her to be the guests of her family to eat. I think she found it humorous that we were in such a small tent. Her extended family lived in a very large tent, along with their animals. Not knowing how far away she lived, we decided to stay where we were.

I had noticed that she was admiring a simple silver ring I was wearing, which I had purchased in Jerusalem. Spontaneously, I removed the ring from my finger and offered it to her. Her eyes filled with tears of joy as she accepted it. She slipped it onto her finger and we laughed, realizing she would have to grow into it.

Suddenly she seemed conflicted. I then realized that my simple gesture had obligated her to give me something in return. Becoming a little anxious, I knew I could not accept a lamb—not in the convent where I was staying! But she glanced down at her wrist, which boasted a copper bracelet, probably her only valuable possession. She pointed to it and then to me. She made gestures, and I understood that her mother had placed it on her wrist when she was small and she had never removed it. Then, when she tried with great difficulty to take it off, it was my turn to be conflicted. I did not want her to feel obligated to give me her bracelet.

After much effort, she twisted the bracelet off and joyfully presented it to me. I knew that culturally it would be an insult not to accept it.

Abruptly my new friend bowed, flashed her lovely smile and called to her sheep, who responded immediately by following her. We watched her until she was out of sight, always calling, herding and caring for her sheep. They were in her strong and capable care.

"Good news of great joy" was announced to shepherds on that hillside of Bethlehem, those shepherds no doubt being much like our exquisite young friend.

Angels Guard the Christ Child

From the time of Jesus' birth, it becomes increasingly obvious that two forces were operating: the mighty angels of God protecting the Son of God, and the evil forces of Satan trying frantically to end His life.

One of the most dangerous threats to Jesus was Herod the Great. He ruled over Jerusalem from 37–4 BC and was king when Jesus was born. Herod was as an ambitious tyrant, utterly ruthless, emotionally unstable and terrified of anyone usurping his power. When the Magi traveled from the east following the star of Bethlehem, they paid Herod a courtesy visit because they had crossed into his territory. They inquired of him, "'Where is the one who has been born king of the Jews? We saw his star in the east and have come to worship him.' When King Herod heard this he was disturbed, and all Jerusalem with him" (Matthew 2:2–3).

Herod, paranoid and murderous, deceived the Magi in order to find where the baby, the "King of the Jews," was being hidden. From the Jewish priests, Herod learned that the Promised One was to be born in Bethlehem, a village about five miles south of Jerusalem in the province of Judea. He sent the Magi on their way with a request to report the

Child's location to him, saying that he, too, wanted to go and worship Him.

The Magi departed and the star continued to guide them to Bethlehem, until it came to rest over the place where Joseph and Mary were staying. Sometimes Scripture refers to angels as stars. I often wonder if this guiding star was in fact a luminous and brilliant angel.

The Magi were men of wealth, power and prestige. Upon finding this infant King, they were overcome with wonder and joy. Their response was to kneel and worship Him. They presented Jesus with gifts—gold, incense and myrrh—the provision that His parents would need for the next part of their journey.

In another dramatic intervention, an angel of the Lord warned the Magi in a dream not to report to Herod, but instead to return home by another route. Following the angel's instructions, they slipped away undetected by Herod's spies.

Herod's reaction underscores once again his ruthless character. "When Herod realized that he had been outwitted by the Magi, he was furious, and he gave orders to kill all the boys in Bethlehem and its vicinity who were two years old and under" (Matthew 2:16).

Without warning, Herod's soldiers carried out what to this day is called "the massacre of the innocents." Thus followed the tragic results of one man's tyranny: "A voice is heard in Ramah, weeping and great mourning, Rachel weeping for her children and refusing to be comforted, because they are no more" (Matthew 2:18).

The very night before this tragedy, an angel appeared to Joseph in a dream and said, "Arise," a command that called for immediate action. The angel told Joseph to take Jesus and Mary and flee to Egypt, one hundred miles to the south, and to remain there until the angel spoke to him again. The angel then revealed that Herod was going to search for the Child to kill Him. So Joseph took his family out of Bethlehem under the cover of darkness.

The command from the angel ran counter to the logic of staying in Bethlehem where family could help them. Remarkably, Joseph was completely compliant to the angel's instructions. In this extremely dangerous situation, Joseph relied on God, showing no hesitation in his trust and obedience.

Bible scholars agree that they did not stay in Egypt long, because Herod died a short time later. Following Herod's death, an angel appeared to Joseph in yet another dream and said, "Get up, take the child and his mother and go to the land of Israel, for those who were trying to take the child's life are dead" (Matthew 2:20). Joseph did as the angel commanded him.

After Herod died, his son Archelaus ruled over Judea. Joseph was afraid he might also want to harm the Child. Once again, an angel was sent to give God's instructions. "Having been warned in a dream, [Joseph] withdrew to the district of Galilee, and he went and lived in a town called Nazareth" (Matthew 2:22–23). Mary and Joseph must have been extremely relieved to return home to Nazareth, where they could raise Jesus in safety.

The Bible reveals little about the following "hidden years" of Jesus. We are told only that as He grew, He was filled with wisdom. There is only one major glimpse of Jesus, at age twelve (see Luke 2:41–51).

Jesus' next public appearance was at age thirty when He came to John the Baptist at the Jordan River to be baptized.

After Jesus was baptized and rose out of the water, He began praying. As He prayed, two supernatural events occurred. First, heaven opened and the Holy Spirit descended on Jesus in the form of a dove. Then out of heaven a voice said to Him, "You are my Son, whom I love; with you I am well pleased" (Luke 3:22).

The infilling of the Holy Spirit and God's proclamation of love ignited a supernatural passion in Jesus. His love and obedience to His heavenly Father created an unmatchable, powerful force of healing, love and forgiveness in everything Jesus said and did over the next three years as He moved in the power of the Holy Spirit.

Angels with Jesus in the Wilderness

God's words to Jesus proclaimed to the world and to the domain of Satan in a separate dimension that the Son, the Messiah, had arrived. All of heaven and hell were now on full alert! After Jesus' baptism, the Holy Spirit compelled Him to go into the wilderness, where He prayed and fasted for forty days.

During Jesus' time in the wilderness, Satan approached Him three times, testing and tempting Him to sin. In the full account given in Matthew 4, Jesus ended the battle by declaring, "Away from me, Satan! For it is written, 'Worship the Lord your God, and serve him only.' Then the devil left him, and angels came and attended him" (Matthew 4:10–11).

Satan was not a mere demon, but the lord of the demonic realm. This is his first appearance in the gospel accounts but not his first encounter with Jesus or His holy angels. The first confrontation was in heaven. When God created the angels, they dwelt in loving unity with Him until Satan's rebellion. Satan had been a mighty cherub, one of the highest orders of angels.

Jesus carries all power and authority over the enemy. In the wilderness, when Jesus ordered Satan to leave Him, Satan had to obey His command. Scripture stresses, however, that Satan left Jesus *for a time*. He would return again and again in an attempt to challenge Jesus concerning the will of God.

So it was angels who attended to Jesus. "He was with the wild animals, and angels attended him" (Mark 1:13). Just as an angel prepared food for Elijah to strengthen him, angels met Jesus' needs at a time when He was weakened by a forty-day fast. In addition to the sustenance, they strengthened and encouraged Jesus for the task ahead.

Angels and the Ministry Years of Jesus

Having overcome the enemy, strengthened by angels, Jesus emerged from the wilderness in the *power* of the Spirit. At that point He began His earthly ministry.

One particular story in John 1:43–51 reveals the direct relationship that Jesus had with the angels and how intertwined angelic activity was with Jesus and His disciples.

Jesus had already chosen Andrew and Peter as disciples. Deciding to go to Galilee, He found Philip and simply said, "Follow Me." Philip accepted, then dashed off to find his friend Nathanael. He told Nathanael, "We have found the one Moses wrote about in the Law, and about whom the prophets also wrote—Jesus of Nazareth." Nathanael scoffed at the thought that anything good could come from Nazareth but agreed to meet Jesus.

Jesus saw Nathanael coming and said, "Here is a true Israelite in whom there is nothing false." Nathanael was unimpressed, even a little suspicious.

"How do you know me?" he asked.

Jesus overwhelmed him by saying, "I saw you while you were still under the fig tree before Philip called you."

This astounded Nathanael and caused him to open his heart to Jesus. He proclaimed, "Rabbi, You are the Son of God; You are the King of Israel!"

While Nathanael's mind was still swirling from Jesus' first revelations, Jesus told him that he would see heaven opened, and the angels of God ascending and descending on the Son of Man. In an instant, Nathanael's thoughts would have linked Jesus' bold words to a well-known story from the book of Genesis. There, Jacob saw in a dream a ladder (or a stairway) reaching from earth to heaven, and the angels of God ascending and descending on it (see Genesis 28:12). In this way, Jesus was promising Nathanael—as Jacob was promised—a deeper, new revelation.

Jesus acknowledged the presence, authority and power of angels throughout His ministry. He mentioned angels many times, letting us know their place of prominence in the Kingdom of God. How much of what Jesus tried to tell us have we really understood or believed? Even as He approached the last hours of His life, the angels again returned to His side to comfort and minister to Him.

Angels with Jesus in the Garden of Gethsemane

As I am writing these words about Jesus' Passion—His arrest, trial and crucifixion—it happens to coincide with Holy Week. Along with my usual Lenten preparations, I have been exploring those Scriptures that deal with this holy journey Jesus made. Many details about Jesus emerged: His profound love, His complete obedience and humility, how the angels ministered to Him, and His tender care for His followers.

While living in Jerusalem, I was personally drawn to the Garden of Gethsemane countless times, where I would sit under an ancient, gnarled olive tree to meditate on the love that held Jesus to the path to which His Father called Him.

Jesus had been to the Garden many times to pray (see John 18:2). Tonight was different. Jesus knew it. He had tried to prepare His disciples for the impending desolation that awaited them. Jesus took Peter, James and John a short distance away from the other disciples and shared His agony with them. "My soul is overwhelmed with sorrow to the point of death," He said (Mark 14:34).

We can only imagine the shocked response of His dear friends who had journeyed with Him through trials, miracles, joys and triumphs. They, along with Jesus, felt the ominous cloud looming over them. Then Jesus pleaded with them to stay with Him; He did not want to be left alone. He went a little farther along, prostrated His body before God and prayed with great anguish: "My Father, if it is possible, may this cup [of suffering] be taken from me. Yet not as I will, but as you will" (Matthew 26:39).

As Jesus prayed in great anguish, His distress was so overwhelming that His sweat became great drops of blood falling to the ground. Hematidrosis is a rare medical condition in which sweat and blood mingle when the tiny blood vessels around the sweat glands rupture and effuse into the sweat glands. The cause is almost always extreme anguish. This is what Jesus was experiencing as He accepted His Father's will by relinquishing His own will.

We can sense the agony, sorrow and aloneness of Jesus. Even though His disciples were with Him in the Garden, they could not offer Him the support He needed. They were unable even to cope with their own sorrow and grief.

So Jesus had no human comfort in His greatest hour of anguish.

Into this horrible suffering, the Father mercifully sent a mighty angel to strengthen Jesus for the ordeal ahead. Remember, He was suffering to the point of death. This holy angel carried the remarkable capability to transmit the strength of God's love to His suffering Son. The angel's presence sustained Jesus in His humanity as He accepted the cup of suffering by taking into His sacred being the sins of the world.

According to Matthew, when Jesus was arrested in the Garden, a large crowd armed with swords and clubs arrived with Judas. As a pre-arranged signal given to the soldiers to identify Jesus, Judas kissed Him. As they reached for Jesus, Peter grabbed a sword and cut off the ear of Malchus, the servant of the high priest. Jesus told him to put the sword away, saying that all who live by the sword will die by the sword.

Then He made a remarkable statement: "Do you think I cannot call on my Father, and he will at once put at my disposal more than twelve legions of angels?" (Matthew 26:53). A Roman legion was composed of six thousand soldiers. Nevertheless, swords and clubs were no match for the army of heaven that was available to Jesus.

But Jesus did not call on the warring angels. He knew that suffering was His path to the cross. He said to those arresting Him, "Every day I was with you in the temple courts, and you did not lay a hand on me. But this is your hour—when darkness reigns" (Luke 22:53). The powers of darkness had seized the moment.

Before they led Him away to the Sanhedrin for trial, Jesus displayed His heart and character by performing two acts of unselfish kindness and love. He reached out His healing hands one final time to Malchus and restored his severed ear. Then He turned to the soldiers and implored them to let His disciples go safely. Jesus loved His own to the very end even though He was going to His death. This was remarkably tender care. Jesus was able to say to His Father, "I have not lost one of those that You gave Me."

Following a daybreak trial by the Sanhedrin, Jesus was passed back and forth between Caiaphas (the Jewish high priest), King Herod (Antipas, another son of Herod the Great) and Pontius Pilate (the Roman governor). Pilate ultimately left the decision of Jesus' fate to the people, who cried out, "Crucify Him!" After washing his hands, Pilate reluctantly pronounced the death sentence in the Praetorium (the judgment hall).

Jesus was led away to endure a terrible flogging. He was then crucified on a hill called Golgotha—"The Place of the Skull"—between two thieves. While hanging on that cross for the sins of the world, Jesus was insulted, mocked and ridiculed. Only a few of His followers remained at the cross.

> It was now about the sixth hour, and darkness came over the whole land until the ninth hour, for the sun stopped shining. And the curtain of the temple was torn in two. Jesus called out with a loud voice, "Father, into your hands I commit my spirit." When he had said this, he breathed his last.
>
> Luke 23:44–46

God was completely motivated by love when He sent Jesus to redeem the world through His life, death and resurrection. "God so loved the world that he gave his one and only Son, that whoever believes in him shall not perish but have eternal life" (John 3:16). We cannot understand the depths of the love that made provision for our sins by the blood of the perfect Lamb of God. Nails could not hold God to a cross—only love!

Jesus could have called on the great company of angels that surrounded Him as He suffered on that cross. But He chose not to. We can only imagine the drama unfolding in the supernatural realm: angels watching in horror as Jesus suffered and died. Their Lord and their Master was betrayed, mocked and brutally murdered. The angels were not permitted to intervene, only to observe. The angels had always ministered to Jesus, first in heaven, then from the time of His conception until this horrible yet sacred moment. The great, glorious joy that the angels expressed at His birth was momentarily overshadowed by His agonizing death. But not for long, because indescribable joy was coming!

Angels at the Resurrection

After Jesus' death, Joseph of Arimathea (one of Jesus' secret followers) went to Pilate and requested permission to take Jesus' body off the cross for burial. Pilate granted permission, so Joseph, Nicodemus, Mary (Jesus' mother) and Mary Magdalene, along with some other women, wrapped the broken, bruised body of Jesus in new linen cloth and placed Him in a new tomb hewn out of rock.

The tomb was sealed by a large disc-shaped stone that rolled in a sloped channel to cover the entrance. Since it was the Sabbath, the women planned to return later to anoint the body of Jesus with spices. Embalming was not a Jewish practice; the dead were anointed as a demonstration of devotion and love.

On the third day after Jesus' death, the women returned to the tomb at dawn to anoint Jesus' body. On the way, they wondered who would roll the heavy stone away from the tomb. When they arrived at the tomb, "there was a violent earthquake, for an angel of the Lord came down from heaven and, going to the tomb, rolled back the stone and sat on it. His appearance was like lightning, and his clothes were white as snow" (Matthew 28:2–3).

The women were overwhelmed with awe. The angel then said to the women, "Do not be afraid, for I know that you are looking for Jesus, who was crucified. He is not here; he has risen, just as he said. Come and see the place where he lay" (Matthew 28:5–6).

This mighty, radiant angel from heaven caused the earth to shake, and the terrified Roman guards passed out from their fright. The women stood trembling with fear. The angel's countenance carried the brilliant light of God—the glory of heaven. With a voice like the sound of thunder, he proclaimed the most impassioned news since the angel in Bethlehem had announced the birth of Jesus: "He is not here—He has risen!"

Death, despair and evil were defeated. Hope was restored, and everything Jesus had told them would happen was fulfilled. "Death has been swallowed up in victory" (1 Corinthians 15:54). It is difficult to envision the wild-eyed, passionate response of the women as they peered inside the tomb and saw the linen cloths but not His body, and two angels who announced joyfully, "He is not here—He is risen!"

The angel at the tomb instructed Mary Magdalene to tell the disciples to return to Galilee, and that Jesus would be waiting for them there.

Angels at the Ascension of Jesus

Luke tells us that Jesus "gave many convincing proofs that he was alive. He appeared to them over a period of forty days and spoke about the kingdom of God" (Acts 1:3). Sometimes I wish more had been written about what Jesus did and said during those forty days before His ascension to heaven, but one thing is certain: He continued to encourage, train and equip the disciples in order to spread the Kingdom.

When they were eating one final meal together, Jesus gave them what is perhaps His most significant instruction for the advancement of His Church. Knowing it was time for His departure, He longed to assure them they would not be left alone. He told them to wait for the gift of the Holy Spirit and His power, enabling them to be His witnesses "to the ends of the earth."

Jesus, one last time, led His disciples down through the Kidron Valley, past the Garden of Gethsemane, to the eastern slope of the Mount of Olives near Bethany. The disciples probably were not even aware that this would be their final day with Him.

But now that moment of parting had come. He looked lovingly at each one of His beloved friends; perhaps He embraced and kissed them. Then He raised His hands for one final blessing. Luke tells us, "While he was blessing them, he left them and was taken up into heaven" (Luke 24:51). "And a cloud hid him from their sight" (Acts 1:9).

Jesus ascended to heaven surrounded by a cloud. Billy Graham, in *Angels: God's Secret Agents*, wrote, "Jesus had been accompanied to earth by an angelic host. I believe that the word 'cloud' suggests that angels had come to escort him back to the right hand of God the Father."

Glory clouds are mentioned throughout the Bible and usually indicate a powerful presence of God's radiant glory. In the book of Ezekiel, for instance, "the glory of the LORD rose from above the cherubim and moved to the threshold of the temple. The cloud filled the temple, and the court was full of the radiance of the glory of the LORD" (Ezekiel 10:4). Jesus was being lifted—escorted by multitudes of dazzling, brilliant angels ushering Him into the presence of God's glory, where innumerable hosts of heaven welcomed His return. He did not simply disappear; He moved into another dimension—the Kingdom of God.

The disciples were stunned by His sudden departure and stood staring into the sky, when they became aware of *two men* standing near them dressed in white.

"Men of Galilee," they said, "why do you stand here looking into the sky? This same Jesus, who has been taken from you into heaven, will come back in the same way you have seen him go into heaven" (Acts 1:11). Two angels were sent by God to bring overwhelming good news—Jesus will return!

Suddenly they remembered the words of Jesus when He was teaching about the end of the age: "At that time they will see the Son of Man coming in a cloud with power and great glory" (Luke 21:27). At His Second Coming, Jesus will also return in a cloud of glory. The disciples were overcome with joy and began to worship Him—all that He had told them had come to pass. "And surely I am with you always," He promised, "to the very end of the age" (Matthew 28:20).

9

Angels and the Spread of the Gospel

Therefore, since we are surrounded by such a great cloud of witnesses . . .

Hebrews 12:1

Following the ascension of Jesus and Pentecost, the early Church was established. Luke, the author of the book of Acts, gives us a careful historical account of the first thirty years of the Church. Within this dramatic book, we witness trials, conversions, healings, voyages, disputes, imprisonments and the works of angels. Jesus had relied on angels during His earthly ministry, and He passed on that rich legacy to His apostles and disciples.

Thus, the early Christians understood that angels are ministering spirits sent to serve those who will inherit salvation (see Hebrews 1:14). Seeing angels seemed to be a common occurrence, and believers had a deep appreciation and respect for angelic ministry in their daily lives. Just the opposite seems to be the case today. Mention angelic assistance even to most Christians and you will probably see surprised reactions!

But they are among us, and encounters with them today are just as dramatic as they were in the days of the early Church. In this chapter we will look at a number of stories from the book of Acts, interspersed with stories of angels continuing their faithful ministry among us, continuing to help believers advance God's Kingdom.

The Apostles' Jailbreak

As a result of the miraculous signs and wonders performed by the twelve apostles (another disciple had been chosen to replace Judas), thousands in Jerusalem were becoming believers. Before long, the high priest and the Sadducees were filled with jealousy and ordered the arrest of the apostles. They were thrown into the public jail to await trial by the Sanhedrin the following day, but sometime

> during the night an angel of the Lord opened the doors of the jail and brought them out. "Go, stand in the temple courts," he said, "and tell the people the full message of this new life." At daybreak they entered the temple courts, as they had been told, and began to teach.
>
> Acts 5:19–21

Imagine the apostles huddled together, praying for a move of God—and a mighty "angel of the Lord" (this phrase is used five times in Acts) appears to deliver them to go about God's work. The angel not only opened doors that were locked and guarded, but he led them out from their captivity. When the high priest sent for the apostles to be brought to trial, the officers "found the jail securely locked, with the guards standing at the doors" (verse 23). How did the guards miss a mighty, radiant angel and twelve men walking past them?

As the chief priests and the Temple guards were trying to figure out where the apostles were, someone came rushing in and declared that the apostles were teaching in the Temple courts. This is where outrageous freedom and courage meet! After finally being brought to trial, they were admonished to stop teaching about Jesus.

Peter, along with the others, however, proclaimed boldly the truth about Jesus to the high priest and entire Sanhedrin. Keep in mind, these were the same religious leaders who condemned Jesus and called for His crucifixion.

The furious response of all those gathered there was immediate: "Kill them! Silence the message of the Kingdom!" But Gamaliel, a Pharisee, the most well-known teacher of the time, gave a cautious warning: "Leave these men alone! Let them go! For if their purpose or activity is of human origin, it will fail. But if it is from God, you will not be able to stop these men; you will only find yourselves fighting against God" (verses 38–39).

The message of God's beloved Son cannot be silenced, especially in the hearts of those who have been empowered by the Holy Spirit and who have walked with angels. After being flogged and ordered not to speak the name of Jesus, these unstoppable men of God left the Sanhedrin rejoicing. "Day after day, in the temple courts and from house to house, they never stopped teaching and proclaiming the good news that Jesus is the Christ" (verse 42).

Jails and prisons, and angelic deliverance from them, can take many forms. In this next story of a broken young man, we see that angels continue today their ministry of helping captives be set free to declare the Kingdom message.

Angels in the Night

When I was 22, I was in the midst of a divorce and living in my parents' basement apartment. My mother cared for my son while I was at work. Except for my job, my life was a mess. I was abusing alcohol and drugs. Even though I professed to be a Christian, I was just "playing church." My only saving grace was that I had a praying mother.

Every evening after work, my usual routine consisted of smoking pot, going to clubs and hooking up with women. For some reason, one night was different. I had no desire for drugs. I went to the clubs, but could not enjoy being there. The oddest thing of all was that I had no desire to drink alcohol either. I did not think much of it then, but now I know that God was preparing me for an encounter.

I returned home around ten p.m., which was early for me. I turned off the lights as I walked through the house toward my basement apartment. As I moved through the darkness, I saw two angels who looked like very tall men, wearing white robes. Feeling stunned, I walked toward them slowly. The one to my right had long hair that shone like gold and glorious giant wings. He had radiant bronze skin and the brightest, warmest smile.

The other angel had similar wings and bronze skin, but his hair was curly and jet black. They both wore breastplates and carried swords. They appeared as if ready for battle. The dark-haired one spoke to me without opening his mouth and said, "You need to stop what you're doing!" I was so startled that I ran to my room, where I fell to my knees praying.

In time, with God's help, I was able to clean up my life. Eventually I became a pastor.

Thirty-five years after that night, I attended the Christian Healing Ministries' School of Healing Prayer. I have been praying for people since and have seen many healings, both physical and spiritual. One morning I went into the office to speak to a staff member at CHM. Hanging on the wall behind her desk was an icon of an angel that bore an uncanny resemblance to one of the angels who had appeared to me when I was 22. Later, during a prayer session, Judith came to pray for me. As she laid her hands on me, I saw my two angels standing behind her, one on each side of her. As I rested in the Spirit, I cried for joy, for it was reaffirmation from the Lord that He is always faithful.

—Raul Toro

Today Raul is an anointed pastor, serving God by reaching lost, suffering and needy people. How wonderful that God allowed him to see the same two angels that have been with him for more than 35 years!

Peter's Miraculous Rescue from Prison

The account of Peter's arrest and miraculous release in Acts 12 is one of my favorite angel stories in Scripture. The following story illustrates two truths about angels:

1. They are supernaturally empowered by God to accomplish the mission to which He assigns them.
2. The early Church held the belief that every believer has a guardian angel assigned to care for him or her.

During the Feast of Unleavened Bread, King Herod continued his persecution of the Church by killing the apostle James. Seeing that this made him more popular with the Jews, he also had Peter arrested, intending to bring him to trial after Passover. King Herod placed a heavy guard around Peter—four squads of four soldiers each.

That night, while Peter's fellow believers in Jerusalem were praying for his release, a radiant light filled the cell and an angel of the Lord appeared. Peter, bound with chains, was sleeping between two soldiers. The angel hit Peter on the side to wake him up. Suddenly the chains fell off Peter's wrists, and the angel told him to get dressed and follow him. Peter, led by the angel, walked past the two stations of guards without being noticed. When the angel and Peter arrived at the iron gate to the city, it swung open by itself. After going down one street, the angel left Peter standing in amazement. It was at this point that Peter realized he was not simply seeing a vision; God had sent an angel to rescue him from certain death.

Peter rushed to the home of Mary, the mother of Mark, where the believers had gathered to pray for him. This is the place in the story where you can visualize the exchange between Peter, Rhoda and the believers in the house. Peter, looking anxiously over his shoulder for Herod's guards, was standing at the outer door of the home, knocking hurriedly. Rhoda, a hired servant girl, went to answer the door, but recognizing Peter's voice, she became so excited that she ran back into the house without opening it. Now he was really knocking!

Rhoda told the believers, who were on their knees crying out to God for Peter's freedom, that he was at the door. Their first response? "You're out of your mind." So much for active belief that their prayers would be answered! When Rhoda kept insisting it was Peter, what was their second response? "It must be his angel."

This statement shows their ingrained belief that sometimes a person's guardian angel will take on the appearance of that person. All the while, Peter continued tapping at the door. When they finally saw it was really Peter, they were astonished.

As Peter relayed the incredible events that led up to his freedom, I am sure that deep reverence fell over the group, followed by a joyful celebration of God's great provision— through the power of a mighty angel of God.

The next morning, when Herod discovered that Peter had somehow escaped, he cross-examined the guards and ordered that they be executed. Herod's persecution of the early Church surely placed him on dangerous ground with God. One day Herod, dressed in his royal robes, delivered a public address in Caesarea and received adulation from the people, who shouted, "'This is the voice of a god, not of a man.' Immediately, because Herod did not give praise to God, an angel of the Lord struck him down, and he was eaten by worms and died" (Acts 12:22–23).

Yet the Gospel continued to spread.

The darkness that drove Herod continues to war against the increase of God's Kingdom, but God still sends His protective angels to guard and guide—even in the darkest of places, as the following stories show.

Protection in a Dangerous Slum

An enormous squatter's camp, or slum, home to fifty thousand people, known as Mzamom'hle Township, or M-Town, is notorious for being one of the most dangerous slums in South Africa. It has among the highest rates of alcoholism, drug abuse, murder and rape in all of Africa. When I first started ministering in M-Town, I was cautioned against going into the slum.

The following year, though, I met some of the key locals and was assured a measure of security in the "safe" parts of the slum. Our mission hired a pastor, a young Xhosa man by the name of Vuzi, better known to the locals as Chief. While many Xhosa are average height, Chief was tall and imposing, highly respected and a godly man. He was God's provision for us, and we made sure he accompanied us to visit the most needy people. I knew that as the (Christian, female, white) leader of this mission, I was a target for both the enemy and certain people. I had three safety rules: always be out of the slum by dusk; never go off the main roads without a well-respected local, preferably Chief; and never, ever, go into Section H.

Section H is the most dangerous part of M-Town. Most of the residents do not venture out after dark, and even during daylight hours women and children in the area hurry home, locking ramshackle doors tightly behind them. Most of the slum's murders and almost all of the rapes happen there. In addition to its dark spirit, the place has a sinister look. Vigilante justice is meted out in the township, occasionally producing a dismembered body part staked out as a warning. It is a desperate and frightening place to be.

One day I was with a team consisting of a guard and a translator visiting some of the more needy residents. Chief was not with us. We were trying to circumvent Section H, but found ourselves deep in the back trails of the slum. I had been searching for a certain child and thought that I recognized his shack. I ducked inside quickly, and spoke with the solitary old woman in the shack. Not finding the child, I ran out looking for the other team members, but they were nowhere in sight. I prayed for God to lead me out of this dangerous place and asked Him to surround me with His angels. As I rounded a bend, I came face-to-face with a group of the slum's most notorious *tsotsis*, or gangsters, who were armed and drunk. They recognized me and began to call to me. I started running without looking back. I was so thankful to God that He protected me.

The following day I was at our makeshift clinic and saw one of the young tsotsis from the day before. As I approached him, he started to laugh hysterically and told me never to come back to his area. He said, "You are lucky Chief was with you, hey!" I could not believe what I was hearing. "Ja, Chief, man, he was looking very cross that we were shouting at you!" the young man retorted.

Chief had been on the other side of the slum all day, but this tsotsi and his friends had seen Chief with me—and Chief looked angry! God had sent an angel to protect me.

When I told Chief what had happened, he did not bat an eye, but rather asked why I was surprised that God had sent His protection. "This whole place is a spiritual battle," he told me. "All you have to do is lift your eyes to see it. There are angels and demons everywhere, but God has already won."

—Heather Deyo

Angels Stop an Angry Mob

Miss Helen Hornby, a much-loved missionary of the Church of England, worked among the Ibo women in the Owerri District of eastern Nigeria for many years. She was in charge of a school for betrothed girls, where husbands-to-be sent their fiancées to be prepared for marriage and baptism in accordance with the Christian rite. Most of the girls came from pagan homes and had had little exposure to Christianity. Miss Hornby and her assistants taught the students to read the Bible and understand the catechism, and prepared them to make an informed commitment to Christ.

During that time, the people of the Owerri District experienced financial upheaval when the introduction of a new tax coincided with the fall in the export price of palm nut oil, one of Nigeria's main products. To make matters worse, the import price of kerosene, the essential fuel for bush lanterns that provided the sole source of light in most Nigerian homes, rose precipitously. This unfortunate combination of shifting prices and unwanted taxation led to great unrest in the region, culminating in what was

202

known as the "Women's War." A powerful group of
trading women banded together in hostile opposition
to European businesses, institutions and interests,
and their methods of protest became violent as their
numbers grew larger and angrier.

One night, when the Women's War had reached
a fever pitch, a mob of anti-European women approached the missionary compound with the intention of burning the school to the ground. Fearing
violence, Miss Hornby gathered the girls together to
pray for the members of the furious mob who had
converged on the campus, whose roaring threats had
become terrifying to the students and teachers alike.
They continued to pray through the night.

In the midst of this frenzy, all noise outside ceased
suddenly, and it became apparent that the mob was
retreating. Everyone in the house offered thanksgiving to God for answering their frantic prayers. Miss
Hornby sent the girls to bed. She sat and continued
praying, grateful for the preservation of the school
and the lives inside it.

For some years no one knew why the mob had
turned from the school that night. The Women's War
came to an end, and the hostility toward European
things ceased. The school carried on without inter-
ruption, and the district returned to a more peaceful
state.

Two years later, a young woman came to Miss
Hornby's school for training. Just before her baptism, she confessed this to Miss Hornby: "Mother, I
was one of the women who came that night to burn
down your house." Miss Hornby asked the girl why

the mob went away. "We were afraid of the shining ones who stood before your door."

The girl explained that as soon as the mob got close to the house, they saw two tall people there. The sight of them deeply frightened the members of the mob. Not wanting to engage with these beings of light, they retreated into the night.

How encouraging and beautiful it is to know that God's angels sometimes make themselves known in order to protect those who cannot protect themselves!

—Elizabeth M. Wilkinson

I am convinced that angels, although usually invisible to us, are constantly guarding God's servants. Frequently, however, in times of danger, the angels make their appearance known to ward off our enemies.

Three Angels Give Guidance

Angels are directly involved in helping believers advance the Kingdom—whether by offering unseen protection or giving specific directions.

Philip was an evangelist on a mission to spread the word about the Kingdom of God when an angel spoke to him: "Go south to the road—the desert road—that goes down from Jerusalem to Gaza" (Acts 8:26).

Philip followed the orders immediately, and on his way encountered a prominent Ethiopian who was riding in his chariot and reading from the book of Isaiah—specifically, the Messianic prophecy about Jesus. Philip shared the good news of the Gospel with him, and the Ethiopian received Jesus, was baptized and went on his way rejoicing.

An angel also spoke to the apostle Paul, giving him guidance for an arduous journey ahead where he would present a powerful testimony.

Paul, along with other prisoners, was aboard a commercial ship sailing to Rome, where he would stand trial before Caesar. On the way, a violent northeaster, with hurricane-force winds, battered the ship severely for many days. The crew began to throw their cargo and even the ship's tackle overboard—everything possible in order to lighten the ship. Their situation was becoming increasingly desperate. Then in the midst of the raging storm, a mighty angel of God appeared to Paul to bring him words of comfort and encouragement: "Do not be afraid, Paul—no lives will be lost" (see Acts 27:24).

Immediately Paul gathered the terrified men together and shouted over the raging storm that an angel of God had visited him and assured him that not one of them would die. I wonder what kind of reaction that news brought to these seasoned sailors who obviously thought they were all going to perish? Living in Florida, I have been through several northeasters and a few hurricanes. One ripped out two giant oak trees that stood in our front yard and tossed another tree across the roof of our garage. I will never forget the sound and ferocity of that storm. I believe there must have been angels watching over us because our home and our lives were spared.

The 276 men aboard that ship being tossed so fiercely in the sea were spared as well. Finally, on the fourteenth night, the sailors sensed that they were approaching land. Paul emerged as a courageous leader, giving solid direction in how to proceed. Surely angels surrounded that ship, bringing it through the storm; the ship was destroyed but no lives perished, just as the angel had foretold.

As the apostle Peter traveled around the country, he was asked to come to nearby Joppa to a certain home. A beloved disciple named Dorcas had suddenly become ill and died. Dorcas' body had already been prepared for burial, and seeing the disciples' great sorrow at her death, Peter was deeply moved. Sending everyone out of the room, he fell to his knees beside her bed—and he prayed, seeking the will of God. Then he said to the dead woman, "Arise!" Dorcas opened her eyes and was restored to life and to her community!

Peter stayed in Joppa for some time. One day he was summoned to visit a home in Caesarea, not a Christian home, but that of a Roman centurion, a Gentile, Cornelius.

But before Peter would allow himself to enter the home of a Gentile, which was forbidden by Jewish practice, he had to have a change of heart through a supernatural experience. Peter, who had gone up on the roof to pray, fell into a trance and had three visions. Each time he saw heaven open, and a large canvas lowered before him, stretched out by its four corners. The canvas held different kinds of four-footed animals, birds and reptiles that were not kosher. "Then a voice told him, 'Get up, Peter. Kill and eat.' 'Surely not, Lord!' Peter replied. 'I have never eaten anything impure or unclean.' The voice spoke to him a second time, 'Do not call anything impure that God has made clean'" (Acts 10:13–15).

When the vision ended, the men sent by Cornelius appeared at the home where Peter was staying, asking for him to come with them. In the meantime, the Holy Spirit had told Peter that three men were looking for him, and not to hesitate to go with them.

This entire account of Cornelius and Peter had tremendous significance for the young Church. Before this event, no Jew would fellowship with a Gentile because he would be considered unclean. It took, in fact, three visions, along with an angel's voice interpreting the visions, and the Holy Spirit's specific direction before Peter got the message that he was supposed to go with the travelers to the home of Cornelius and share the plan of salvation. Peter, along with some other believers, spent two days traveling the thirty miles from Joppa to Caesarea to the home of Cornelius, who had gathered his entire family and friends to listen to Peter.

As Peter proclaimed the Good News about Jesus, the Holy Spirit came upon all who were listening. The Christians were shocked that the gift of the Holy Spirit had been poured out on Gentiles, who were now praising God and speaking in tongues—as had happened on the day of Pentecost. "Then Peter said, 'Can anyone keep these people from being baptized with water? They have received the Holy Spirit just as we have.' So he ordered that they be baptized in the name of Jesus Christ" (Acts 10:46–48). The Church had just changed radically by welcoming Gentiles to come into the Kingdom.

Angels Still Guide Today

As we continue our work to establish the Kingdom of God on the earth, we can be sure that the power of the Holy Spirit and the supernatural help of God's angels will guide and keep us. These next stories encourage us to do that.

Angels at Vacation Bible School

My ten-year-old grandson Simeon was diagnosed with juvenile type 1 diabetes. Understanding his condition has been difficult for him, and he has had a lot of questions. For a time he questioned if God is even real.

One summer night I took Simeon to vacation Bible school, praying he would have a positive experience. Simeon went into the "encounter room," where children could spend time in prayer. Due to a recent injury, his shoulder was in a brace, so one of the group's members offered to pray for his shoulder. Simeon reported that his shoulder felt completely better afterward.

As Simeon shared with us about what had happened during prayer, he started shaking and crying, telling us that right then he saw an angel in the room. Simeon asked the angel why he had come. The angel said that he was always with Simeon, and he was there to help with his healing.

Simeon then felt coolness on his back and heat on his chest and stomach. He continued trembling for about ten minutes. Simeon described the angel as being a male standing about six-foot-three with dark hair and wearing a white robe with gold trim. He said he was smiling the whole time. What really impressed Simeon was the angel's feathery, silver wings, which were so large they touched the ceiling and walls in the large room.

Then Simeon asked us, "Who is the man in white?" We did not know what he meant, so he described the man to us. Eventually Simeon said that it was Jesus, and that He was there to help us. When he said this, the room filled with a sense of the glory of heaven. One woman dropped to the floor. It was difficult for us to stand. Although Simeon said he could see Jesus' wounds in His hands and feet, His face was so bright he could not look directly at Him. The angel stayed by Jesus all the time. Simeon said Jesus touched him, and that was when the heat and shaking intensified. Despite all this, he said he was not fearful. We went into the sanctuary, and Simeon saw four more angels, which he described in great detail. When he asked them who they were, they said they were protectors.

—Emlee Overall and Randall Martin
(Simeon's mother and grandfather)

Children seem to accept the spiritual realm more easily than adults. It seems that as we age, that ability diminishes. Over the course of time do we slowly start to disregard the spiritual realm around us? Only Simeon could see his angel and Jesus, but family and friends working to help establish the Kingdom of God on earth knew the presence of God was in that place.

An Angel in the Living Room

One Sunday, during lunch, the conversation turned to the subject of angels. Our son, then sixteen years old, was upstairs during this conversation. On his way out he passed through our gathering and, picking up the gist of the chat, said, "We have an angel in this house. He's in the living room."

He explained that one day he was opening the front door when he had an impulse to go into the living room, which he hardly ever frequented. On this occasion, as he entered, he was amazed to see an enormous figure standing as if on guard. He described it almost as tall as the ceiling, burnished and shining. As the father of a teen who had never shown any signs of religious interest, I was a bit skeptical.

Later that same week, a young man came to my wife and me for counseling. This was his fourth session, and as I let him in the front door he turned around and said, "I know that it's right to continue to come see you because on my first visit, I was aware of the presence of an angel standing on the stairs behind you."

My wife and I were also counseling a young woman at this time, and on her next visit to our home, only a few days after this young man's visit, she was halfway through the session when, totally out of context, she said, "I feel safe when I come here because I know that you are both special. You must be, because there is always an angel in the room with us."

Three young people, none of whom knew each other, all gave witness to the presence of an angel in our living room. I have never seen the angel they speak of, but I am nonetheless grateful for his presence.

—Ronald Bisset

The following took place at a Kathryn Kuhlman service in California in 1973. I was excited to read this story among letters sent to Jamie Buckingham, our dear friend. Kathryn Kuhlman was known for her large healing services in the 1960s and 1970s. She was an anointed woman of God who ministered the healing love of God all over the world. I first met Kathryn in Jerusalem, where she ministered to more than five thousand people over the course of two evenings. Many of my friends suffering from serious illnesses were healed during those meetings. I am certain that angels were with her wherever she went.

Seven Dazzling Ministering Angels

When my son was twelve years old, I brought him to a Kathryn Kuhlman service. After some time, I noticed that something had captivated my son's attention. He was looking at an injured young man who was lying on a medical bed.

Suddenly, he said, "Mom, look!"

"Look at what?" I asked.

"All those angels down there."

"Down where?" I replied, feeling excited at the prospect of seeing angels.

"They're standing around that man's bed."

I felt a touch of impatience, because what was obvious to him was invisible to me.

The service was coming to a close, so I suggested that we go and tell the young man.

When we got there a few people were praying for him, so we joined in. The young man's name was David, and he explained he was in a body cast due to a broken pelvis from a car accident.

I told him about my son seeing the angels, and he was overjoyed. David was curious about the angels, so he wrote my son a letter with a list of questions. I asked my son the questions, and wrote down his answers:

Q: How many angels were there?
A: Seven. Two on each side of the bed, one at the foot, one at the head, and one over the top of the bed looking down at him. They were all looking at him.

Q: What were they wearing?
A: They wore long, beautiful, dazzling robes and had beautiful thick wings. I asked him what he meant by *dazzling*. He said "Picture a bright white, the whitest white you can imagine, and multiply that times a hundred."

Q: Did they have distinct facial features?
A: No, I couldn't see their faces because of the glow.

Q: Were they standing on the floor or floating?
A: They were suspended in the air, about four feet away from the bed. They were all bent forward toward him, loving him. I'll never forget it.

After answering the questions, my son added, "Some of the angels' wings were spread, as though they were getting ready to fly, and some hung by their sides. The wings were wavy looking and ivory white. They started at the angels' shoulder blades and went up about a foot above their heads and down to a point about knee level. The angels were all the same size. They never budged from their positions of ministry around David." My son, now grown, has not forgotten any of what he saw that night.

—Evelyn King

The early Church moved in the power of the Holy Spirit and transformed individuals and society. They relied on the direction of God, on visions, on the gifts of the Holy Spirit and on angelic assistance to usher in the Kingdom of God.

Today believers are being called to return to evangelization as it was modeled for us in the early days of the Church. In 2 Timothy 3:3–5, Paul wrote that in the last days people will maintain the form of godliness, but will leave out its real power.

We cannot proclaim the good news of the Gospel without being empowered by the Holy Spirit. The intent of Paul's letters to the early believers was to draw their attention to the cosmic battle that is taking place against evil in the heavenly realm. He is instructing them, and us, that their human resources will not achieve the desired outcome. This battle requires spiritual weapons and the angelic armies of God.

Conclusion

So we fix our eyes not on what is seen, but on
what is unseen. For what is seen is temporary,
but what is unseen is eternal.

2 Corinthians 4:18

I hope that after reading this book filled with the inspired
true-life stories of angelic encounters, you have come to realize that angels are intimately and actively involved in your
life and in the restoration of the Kingdom of God. As God
opens your heart and eyes to the dynamic spiritual realm,
you might behold visions, angels and other aspects of God's
majestic realm: "For now we see through a glass, darkly; but
then face to face: now I know in part; but then shall I know
even as also I am known" (1 Corinthians 13:12 KJV).

Billy Graham, in *Angels: God's Secret Agents*, says that

our eyes are not constructed to see angels ordinarily anymore
than we can see the dimensions of a nuclear field, the structure of atoms, or the electricity that flows through copper

215

wiring. Our ability to sense is limited, but some animals are adapted to see into the darkness—things that escape our attention. So why should we think it strange if our eyes fail to perceive the evidences of angelic presence? Could it be that God granted Balaam and his donkey a new optical capacity to view the angel?

The account of Balaam and his donkey in Scripture is a humorous story about a pagan prophet riding his donkey on a journey. Three times the donkey stops walking when he sees an angel of the Lord blocking their path and three times Balaam beats him for stopping. Finally the Lord opens the donkey's mouth to speak to Balaam, and the donkey asks why he is being beaten. The donkey not only sees the angel but speaks! "Then the LORD opened Balaam's eyes, and he saw the angel of the LORD standing in the road with his sword drawn. So he bowed low and fell facedown" (Numbers 22:31). Balaam, a well-known seer, is blind to the spiritual reality of the angel, but his donkey sees the angel immediately. It would seem that the greater miracle is that God opened the eyes of a pagan prophet to see, but the donkey's gifts are incredible, too.

When we pray for God to open our eyes to see into the spiritual realm, sometimes God allows us to see angels standing guard around us. We discover that the angels have been there all along in a different dimension. God graciously allows us to see, to feel and to experience His Kingdom when He deems it necessary. Remember Jesus' words: "I tell you the truth, you shall see heaven open, and the angels of God ascending and descending on the Son of Man" (John 1:51).

C. S. Lewis, the great English writer, said that heaven and all that it contains is in another dimension. Jesus taught that the Kingdom of God or Kingdom of heaven is all around us and will be in us. Primitive peoples looked to the sky to find God. Jesus focused on the Kingdom growing within, like yeast or a seed.

One of my mentors in my spiritual journey was the Reverend Jamie Buckingham. I first met him when he came to Narkis Street Baptist Church in Jerusalem and taught about the Kingdom of God. His teaching had a profound influence on my understanding of the supernatural realm of the Holy Spirit, angels and demons. Jamie, who traveled extensively, said that people in so-called primitive cultures often have a deeper understanding of the spiritual dimension than those in Western cultures. They are more open to visions, dreams and supernatural communication. In his book *Risky Living: Keys to Inner Healing* (Logos, 1976), Jamie outlines the three sources of knowledge as described in the ancient works of Plato.

> The first source of knowledge [is] the five senses: taste, hearing, sight, touch and smell.
>
> A second source of knowledge is reason. Reason is the thing that sets us above all the other creatures. It enables us to reach logical conclusions.
>
> A third source of knowledge is what Plato called "divine madness," referring to the world of spiritual communication. Here a person receives knowledge neither through the senses nor through the mind. It comes from the Source of Power to our spirit. Some might call it intuition, others inspiration.

Jamie continues: "Later, Aristotle, who was Plato's disciple, eliminated the third or supernatural source. Unfortunately much of what we experience in the Western world is based on Aristotle's philosophy."

Regrettably, the world we live in—and even the Church—has evolved to accept only those things that can be proven through reason and our senses. The larger spiritual dimension of the Holy Spirit, the voice of God, angels and demons is largely doubted if not entirely discredited. If you do not believe me, try saying at your next social gathering, "God told me . . ." Knowing looks of surprise and amusement will pass around the group. The primary reason people who have had angelic encounters are often afraid to talk about them is because "you might think I'm crazy." This is tragic. The early Church relied on the direction of God, on visions, on dreams, on the gifts of the Holy Spirit and on angelic help. They also understood and accepted their need for protection from the fallen angels or demons.

I remember visiting Mother Basilea Schlink's community in Darmstadt, Germany, when I was studying Christian communities. She founded the Evangelical Sisterhood of Mary, a Protestant group of believers seeking to serve God through community. She, too, spoke of the supernatural world in everyday terms. In *The Unseen World of Angels and Demons* (Lakeland, 1985), she wrote:

> The angels of God are bright and shining beings, emanating light and mirroring the glory of God. Often when angels appear visibly, people fall to the ground, overwhelmed by their radiance, grandeur and power. In the angels they encounter something of God's holiness. Today we have forgotten what an elevated position the angels have before God. What a source of strength and courage it would be for us to know that the holy armies of heaven, the angels, are battling on behalf of us weak mortals!

God created the mighty angels and sends them to be loyal companions and faithful friends on your life journey. Their ministry to you is an incredible gift from your loving heavenly

Father. At the beginning of each day it would be wise to pray that the Holy Spirit would fill the day with God's power. Many people ask us for prayers to guide them in their spiritual journey. The following is a prayer that might be helpful to you and your family:

Dear Lord,

I believe that You created me to know and love You in an ongoing, ever-changing intimate relationship. You have a plan and purpose for me—show me Your path for my life.

My concerns are deeply important to You. Please grace me to know that in everything I am going through I am never alone—You are always with me. And Your mighty angels accompany me through every trial and temptation to keep my feet from stumbling.

Thank You for sending Your holy angels to protect me and my loved ones. Thank You that they guide, comfort, enlighten and uplift my soul to keep my eyes on You and Your eternal Kingdom.

Please fill me with Your Holy Spirit. Fill my mind with Your light, my will with Your strength, my body and emotions with Your health and healing power. Fill my entire being with Your life and love. Let me become like You, Jesus, so my life will reflect Your radiant presence. Amen.

Judith MacNutt, president and co-founder of Christian Healing Ministries in Jacksonville, Florida, holds a master's degree in psychology from Eastern Kentucky University and is a licensed psychotherapist in Florida. Early in her career she discovered the need to address her clients' spiritual needs as well as the psychological issues. After working in psychiatric hospitals in Boston and Kentucky, Judith moved to Jerusalem, where she directed a house of prayer, Jerusalem House.

After returning to the U.S., Judith established Christian Counseling Services in Clearwater, Florida, integrating her work as a psychotherapist with healing prayer. She married Francis MacNutt in 1980, and together they founded Christian Healing Ministries. They have traveled extensively together and co-authored the book *Praying for Your Unborn Child* (Hodder and Stoughton, Ltd., 1988). Judith also authored *Angels Are for Real* (Chosen, 2012). Judith continues to travel and speak about the power of healing prayer. Judith and Francis live in Jacksonville, Florida, and have two adult children, Rachel and David.

If you have experienced the help and intervention of angels, Judith would love to hear from you. Please send your story to her at angelstories@christianhealingmin.org. Include your name, address, phone number and email address in case Judith would like to contact you about using your story as an illustration.

Don't Miss Judith's Bestselling Book, *Angels Are for Real*!

You've read the incredible stories— now see what the Bible has to say about these heavenly beings!

As you've seen, angels are a vital part in God's Kingdom. In this accessible, comprehensive and encouraging guide, Judith MacNutt shows why, offering insight and answers as she reveals what the Bible says about

- what angels look like
- what they do
- why they are important in believers' lives
- the heavenly hierarchy
- what fallen angels are
- and more

When you begin to grasp the importance of angels to God—and your very own life—you will better understand God's power and His extraordinary love for you.

Angels Are for Real by Judith MacNutt

✓Chosen